RHYMES OF CHILDHOOD

RHYMES OF CHILDHOOD

JAMES WHITCOMB RILEY

Fredonia Books
Amsterdam, The Netherlands

Rhymes of Childhood

by
James Whitcomb Riley

ISBN: 1-4101-0698-5

Copyright © 2004 by Fredonia Books

Reprinted from the 1900 edition

Fredonia Books
Amsterdam, The Netherlands
http://www.fredoniabooks.com

All rights reserved, including the right to reproduce this book, or portions thereof, in any form.

In order to make original editions of historical works available to scholars at an economical price, this facsimile of the original edition of 1900 is reproduced from the best available copy and has been digitally enhanced to improve legibility, but the text remains unaltered to retain historical authenticity.

TO THE LITTLE NEPHEW
HENRY EDMUND EITEL

PREFATORY NOTE

In presenting herein the child dialect upon an equal footing with the proper or more serious English, the conscientious author feels it neither his desire nor province to offer excuse.

Wholly simple and artless, Nature's children oftentimes seem the more engaging for their very defects of speech and general deportment. We need worry very little for their futures since the All-Kind Mother has them in her keep.

It is just and good to give the elegantly trained and educated child a welcome hearing. It is no less just and pleasant to admit his homely but wholesome-hearted little brother to our interest and love.   J. W. R.

CONTENTS

RHYMES OF CHILDHOOD

	PAGE
The Rider of the Knee	2
A Boy's Mother	219
A Child's Home—Long Ago	186
An Impetuous Resolve	178
A Nonsense Rhyme	167
A Mother-Song	53
A Passing Hail	191
A Prospective Glimpse	161
A Sleeping Beauty	210
A Sudden Shower	179
At Aunty's House	213
Babe Herrick	120
Babyhood	105
Baby's Dying	93
Billy Could Ride	199
Billy Goodin'	189
Busch and Tommy	117
Christine Braibry	78
Christmas Afterthought	27
Curly Locks	163
Dusk-Song—The Beetle	103
Envoy	232
Exceeding All	69
Grandfather Squeers	124
Guiney-Pigs	115

CONTENTS

	PAGE
HE CALLED HER IN	151
HIS CHRISTMAS SLED	118
HONEY DRIPPING FROM THE COMB	198
IN SWIMMING-TIME	220
IN THE NIGHT	55
JACK-IN-THE-BOX	37
JOHN TARKINGTON JAMESON	113
LAWYER AND CHILD	68
LITTLE GIRLY-GIRL	35
LITTLE JOHNTS'S CHRIS'MUS	141
LITTLE MANDY'S CHRISTMAS-TREE	136
LONGFELLOW'S LOVE FOR THE CHILDREN	48
MABEL	33
MAX AND JIM	107
McFEETERS' FOURTH	133
MOTHER GOOSE	19
NAUGHTY CLAUDE	170
OLD MAN'S NURSERY RHYME	96
ON THE SUNNY SIDE	43
OUR HIRED GIRL	229
PANSIES	13
PRIOR TO MISS BELLE'S APPEARANCE	193
SHE "DISPLAINS" IT	202
SONG—FOR NOVEMBER	196
SOME SCATTERING REMARKS OF BUB'S	7
THAT-AIR YOUNG-UN	88
THE ALL-GOLDEN	45
THE BOY-FRIEND	157
THE BOY LIVES ON OUR FARM	225
THE BOYS	94
THE BOYS' CANDIDATE	149
THE BROOK-SONG	85
THE BUMBLEBEE	150

CONTENTS

	PAGE
THE CHRISTMAS LONG AGO	30
THE CIRCUS-DAY PARADE	108
THE DAYS GONE BY	25
THE DREAM OF THE LITTLE PRINCESS	70
THE FISHING PARTY	223
THE FUNNIEST THING IN THE WORLD	140
THE FUNNY LITTLE FELLOW	56
THE HAPPY LITTLE CRIPPLE	20
THE HUNTER BOY	181
THE JOLLY MILLER	204
THE LAND OF THUS-AND-SO	121
THE LAND OF USED-TO-BE	74
THE LITTLE COAT	65
THE LITTLE-RED-APPLE TREE	5
THE LITTLE TINY KICKSHAW	129
THE LUGUBRIOUS WHING-WHANG	130
THE MAN IN THE MOON	183
THE NINE LITTLE GOBLINS	62
THE OLD HAY-MOW	111
THE OLD, OLD WISH	171
THE OLD TRAMP	162
THE ORCHARD LANDS OF LONG AGO	147
THE PET COON	165
THE PIXY PEOPLE	8
THE PRAYER PERFECT	52
THE PREACHER'S BOY"	173
THE RAGGEDY MAN	217
THE ROBINS' OTHER NAME	28
THE RUNAWAY BOY	227
THE SONG OF YESTERDAY	99
THE SQUIRT-GUN UNCLE MAKED ME	83
THE WAY THE BABY CAME	17
THE WAY THE BABY SLEPT	203

CONTENTS

	PAGE
The Way the Baby Woke	132
The Whitheraways	215
The Youthful Press	87
Time of Clearer Twitterings	39
To Hattie—On her Birthday	29
Tommy Smith	3
Uncle Sidney	12
Uncle Sidney's Views	59
Uninterpreted	18
Waitin' fer the Cat to Die	14
When Early March Seems Middle May	60
When Our Baby Died	77
When the World Bu'sts Through	159
Winter Fancies	49
With the Current	207

RHYMES OF CHILDHOOD

THE RIDER OF THE KNEE

*Knightly Rider of the Knee
Of Proud-prancing Unclery!
Gaily mount, and wave the sign
Of that mastery of thine.*

*Pat thy steed and turn him free,
Knightly Rider of the Knee!
Sit thy charger as a throne—
Lash him with thy laugh alone:*

*Sting him only with the spur
Of such wit as may occur,
Knightly Rider of the Knee,
In thy shriek of ecstasy.*

*Would, as now, we might endure,
Twain as one—thou miniature
Ruler, at the rein of me—
Knightly Rider of the Knee!*

TOMMY SMITH

Dimple-cheeked and rosy-lipped,
With his cap-rim backward tipped
Still in fancy I can see
Little Tommy smile on me—
        Little Tommy Smith.

Little unsung Tommy Smith—
Scarce a name to rhyme it with;
Yet most tenderly to me
Something sings unceasingly—
        Little Tommy Smith.

On the verge of some far land
Still forever does he stand,
With his cap-rim rakishly
Tilted; so he smiles on me—
        Little Tommy Smith.

TOMMY SMITH

Elder-blooms contrast the grace
Of the rover's radiant face—
Whistling back, in mimicry,
"Old—Bob—White!" all liquidly-
      Little Tommy Smith.

O my jaunty statuette
Of first love, I see you yet,
Though you smile so mistily,
It is but through tears I see,
      Little Tommy Smith.

But, with crown tipped back behind
And the glad hand of the wind
Smoothing back your hair, I see
Heaven's best angel smile on me,—
      Little Tommy Smith.

THE LITTLE-RED-APPLE TREE

The Little-red-apple Tree!—
    O the Little-red-apple Tree!
When I was the little-est bit of a boy
    And you were a boy with me!
The bluebird's flight from the topmost boughs
    And the boys up there—so high
That we rocked over the roof of the house
    And whooped as the winds went by!

Hey! The Little-red-apple Tree!
    With the garden-beds below,
And the old grape-arbor so welcomely
    Hiding the rake and hoe!
Hiding, too, as the sun dripped through
    In spatters of wasted gold,
Frank and Amy away from you
    And me in the days of old!

THE LITTLE-RED-APPLE TREE

The Little-red-apple Tree!—
    In the edge of the garden-spot,
Where the apples fell so lavishly
    Into the neighbor's lot;—
So do I think of you alway,
    Brother of mine, as the tree,—
Giving the ripest wealth of your love
    To the world as well as me.

Ho! The Little-red-apple Tree!
    Sweet as its juiciest fruit
Spanged on the palate spicily,
    And rolled o'er the tongue to boot,
Is the memory still and the joy
    Of the Little-red-apple Tree,
When I was the little-est bit of a boy
    And you were a boy with me!

SOME SCATTERING REMARKS
OF BUB'S

W‍UNST I took our pepper-box lid
An' cut little pie-dough biscuits, I did,
An' cooked 'em on our stove one day
When our hired girl she said I may.

Honey's the *goodest* thing—Oo-*ooh!*
An' blackburry-pies is goodest, too!
But wite hot biscuits, ist soakin' wet
Wiv tree-mullasus, is goodest yet!

Miss Maimie she's my Ma's friend,—an'
She's purtiest girl in all the lan'!—
An' sweetest smile an' voice an' face—
An' eyes ist looks like p'serves tas'e'!

I *ruther* go to the Circus-show;
But, 'cause my *parunts* told me so,
I ruther go to the Sund'y School,
'Cause there I learn the goldun rule.

Say, Pa,—what *is* the goldun rule
'At's allus at the Sund'y School?

THE PIXY PEOPLE

It was just a very
   Merry fairy dream!—
All the woods were airy
   With the gloom and gleam
Crickets in the clover
   Clattered clear and strong,
And the bees droned over
   Their old honey-song!

In the mossy passes,
   Saucy grasshoppers
Leaped about the grasses
   And the thistle-burs;
And the whispered chuckle
   Of the katydid
Shook the honeysuckle-
   Blossoms where he hid.

THE PIXY PEOPLE

Through the breezy mazes
   Of the lazy June,
Drowsy with the hazes
   Of the dreamy noon,
Little Pixy people
   Winged above the walk,
Pouring from the steeple
   Of a mullein-stalk.

One—a gallant fellow—
   Evidently King,—
Wore a plume of yellow
   In a jewelled ring
On a pansy bonnet,
   Gold and white and blue,
With the dew still on it,
   And the fragrance, too.

One—a dainty lady,—
   Evidently Queen—
Wore a gown of shady
   Moonshine and green,

THE PIXY PEOPLE

With a lace of gleaming
   Starlight that sent
All the dewdrops dreaming
   Everywhere she went.

One wore a waistcoat
   Of rose-leaves, out and in;
And one wore a faced-coat
   Of tiger-lily-skin;
And one wore a neat coat
   Of palest galingale;
And one a tiny street-coat,
   And one a swallow-tail.

And Ho! sang the King of them,
   And Hey! sang the Queen;
And round and round the ring of them
   Went dancing o'er the green;
And Hey! sang the Queen of them,
   And Ho! sang the King—
And all that I had seen of them
   —Wasn't anything!

THE PIXY PEOPLE

It was just a very
   Merry fairy dream!—
All the woods were airy
   With the gloom and gleam
Crickets in the clover
   Clattered clear and strong,
And the bees droned over
   Their old honey-song!

UNCLE SIDNEY

Sometimes, when I bin bad,
   An' Pa "currecks" me nen,
An' Uncle Sidney he comes here,
   I'm allus good again;

'Cause Uncle Sidney says,
   An' takes me up an' smiles,—
The goodest mens they is ain't good
   As baddest little childs!

PANSIES

Pansies! Pansies! How I love you, pansies!
  Jaunty-faced, laughing-lipped and dewy-eyed
      with glee;
Would my song but blossom in little five-leaf
      stanzas
                As delicate in fancies
                    As your beauty is to me!

But my eyes shall smile on you, and my hands in-
      fold you,
  Pet, caress, and lift you to the lips that love
      you so,
That, shut ever in the years that may mildew or
      mould you,
                My fancy shall behold you
                    Fair as in the long ago.

WAITIN' FER THE CAT TO DIE

Lawzy! don't I rickollect
   That-air old swing in the lane!
Right and proper, I expect,
   Old times *can't* come back again;
But I want to state, ef they
Could come back, and I could say
What *my* pick'ud be, i jing!
I'd say, Gimme the old swing
'Nunder the old locus'-trees
On the old place, ef you please!—
Danglin' there with half-shet eye,
Waitin' fer the cat to die!

I'd say, Gimme the old gang
   O' barefooted, hungry, lean,
Ornry boys you want to hang
   When you're growed up twic't as mean!

WAITIN' FER THE CAT TO DIE

The old gyarden-patch, the old
Truants, and the stuff we stol'd!
The old stompin'-groun', where we
Wore the grass off, wild and free
As the swoop o' the old swing,
Where we ust to climb and cling,
And twist roun', and fight, and lie—
Waitin' fer the cat to die!

'Pears like I 'most allus could
   Swing the highest of the crowd—
Jes sail up there tel I stood
   Downside-up, and screech out loud,—
Ketch my breath, and jes drap back
Fer to let the old swing slack,
Yit my towhead dippin' still
In the green boughs, and the chill
Up my backbone taperin' down,
With my shadder on the groun'
Slow and slower trailin' by—
Waitin' fer the cat to die!

WAITIN' FER THE CAT TO DIE

Now my daughter's little Jane's
   Got a kind o' baby-swing
On the porch, so's when it rains
   She kin play there—little thing!
And I'd limped out t'other day
With my old cheer thisaway,
Swingin' *her* and rockin' too,
Thinkin' how *I* ust to do
At *her* age, when suddenly,
"Hey, Gran'pap!" she says to me,
"Why you rock so slow?" . . . Says I
"Waitin' fer the cat to die!"

THE WAY THE BABY CAME

O THIS is the way the baby came:
  Out of the night as comes the dawn;
Out of the embers as the flame;
  Out of the bud the blossom on
The apple-bough that blooms the same
  As in glad summers dead and gone—
With a grace and beauty none could name
O this is the way the baby came!

UNINTERPRETED

Supinely we lie in the grove's shady greenery,
  Gazing, all dreamy-eyed, up through the trees,—
And as to the sight is the heavenly scenery,
  So to the hearing the sigh of the breeze.

We catch but vague rifts of the blue through the wavering
  Boughs of the maples; and, like undefined,
The whispers and lisps of the leaves, faint and quavering,
  Meaningless falter and fall on the mind.

The vine, with its beauty of blossom, goes rioting
  Up by the casement, as sweet to the eye
As the trill of the robin is restful and quieting
  Heard in a drowse with the dawn in the sky.

And yet we yearn on to learn more of the mystery—
  We see and we hear, but forever remain
Mute, blind and deaf to the ultimate history
  Born of a rose or a patter of rain.

MOTHER GOOSE

Dear Mother Goose! most motherly and dear
    Of all good mothers who have laps wherein
    We children nestle safest from all sin,—
I cuddle to thy bosom, with no fear
To there confess that though thy cap be queer,
    And thy curls gimlety, and thy cheeks thin,
    And though the winkered mole upon thy chin
Tickles thy very nose-tip,—still to hear
    The jolly jingles of mine infancy
Crooned by thee, makes mine eager arms, as now,
    To twine about thy neck, full tenderly
Drawing the dear old face down, that thy brow
    May dip into my purest kiss, and be
    Crowned ever with the baby-love of me.

THE HAPPY LITTLE CRIPPLE

I'M thist a little crippled boy, an' never goin' to grow
An' git a great big man at all!—'cause Aunty told me so.
When I was thist a baby onc't I falled out of the bed
An' got "The Curv'ture of the Spine"—'at's what the Doctor said.
I never had no Mother nen—fer my Pa runned away
An' dassn't come back here no more—'cause he was drunk one day
An' stobbed a man in thish-ere town, an' couldn't pay his fine!
An' nen my Ma she died—an' I got "Curv'ture of the Spine"!

THE HAPPY LITTLE CRIPPLE

I'm nine years old! An' you can't guess how
    much I weigh, I bet!—
Last birthday I weighed thirty-three!—An' I weigh
    thirty yet!
I'm awful little fer my size—I'm purt' nigh lit-
    tler nan
Some babies is!—an' neighbors all calls me "The
    Little Man"!
An' Doc one time he laughed an' said: "I 'spect,
    first think you know,
You'll have a little spike-tail coat an' travel with
    a show!"
An' nen I laughed—till I looked round an' Aunty
    was a-cryin'—
Sometimes she acts like that, 'cause I got "Curv'-
    ture of the Spine"!

I set—while Aunty's washin'—on my little long-
    leg stool,
An' watch the little boys an' girls a-skippin' by
    to school;
An' I peck on the winder, an' holler out an' say:
"Who wants to fight The Little Man 'at dares you
    all to-day?"

THE HAPPY LITTLE CRIPPLE

An' nen the boys climbs on the fence, an' little
    girls peeks through,
An' they all says: "'Cause you're so big, you
    think we're 'feard o' you!"
An' nen they yell, an' shake their fist at me, like
    I shake mine—
They're thist in fun, you know, 'cause I got
    "Curv'ture of the Spine"!

At evening, when the ironin's done, an' Aunty's
    fixed the fire,
An' filled an' lit the lamp, an' trimmed the wick
    an' turned it higher,
An' fetched the wood all in fer night, an' locked
    the kitchen door,
An' stuffed the old crack where the wind blows in
    up through the floor—
She sets the kittle on the coals, an' biles an' makes
    the tea,
An' fries the liver an' the mush, an' cooks a egg
    fer me;
An' sometimes—when I cough so hard—her elder-
    berry wine
Don't go so bad fer little boys with "Curv'ture of
    the Spine"!

THE HAPPY LITTLE CRIPPLE

An' nen when she putts me to bed—an' 'fore she
    does she's got
My blanket-nighty, 'at she maked, all good an'
    warm an' hot,
Hunged on the rocker by the fire,—she sings me
    hymns, an' tells
Me 'bout The Good Man—yes, an' Elves, an'
    Old Enchanter spells;
An' tells me more—an' more—an' more!—tel I'm
    asleep, purt' nigh—
Only I thist set up ag'in an' kiss her when she cry,
A-tellin' on 'bout *some* boy's Angel-mother—an'
    it's *mine!* . . .
My *Ma's* a *Angel*—but *I'm* got "The Curv'ture
    of the Spine"!

But Aunty's all so childish-like on my account,
    you see,
I'm 'most afeared she'll be took down—an' 'at's
    what bothers *me!*—
'Cause ef my good old Aunty ever would git sick
    an' die,

THE HAPPY LITTLE CRIPPLE

I don't know what she'd do in Heaven—till *I*
　　come, by an' by:—
Fer she's so ust to all my ways, an' ever'thing,
　　you know,
An' no one there like me, to nurse an' worry over
　　so!—
'Cause all the little childerns there's so straight an'
　　strong an' fine,
They's nary angel 'bout the place with "Curv'-
　　ture of the Spine"!

NOTE.—The word "thist," as used in foregoing lines, is an occasional childish pronunciation evolved from the word "just"—a word which in child vernacular has manifold supplanters,—such as "jus," "jes," "des," "jis," "dis," "jist," "dist," "ist," and even "gist," with hard *g* In "thist," as above, sound "th" as in the word "the."

THE DAYS GONE BY

O THE days gone by! O the days gone by!
The apples in the orchard, and the pathway through the rye;
The chirrup of the robin, and the whistle of the quail
As he piped across the meadows sweet as any nightingale;
When the bloom was on the clover, and the blue was in the sky,
And my happy heart brimmed over, in the days gone by.

In the days gone by, when my naked feet were tripped
By the honeysuckle tangles where the water-lilies dipped,

THE DAYS GONE BY

And the ripples of the river lipped the moss along
> the brink
Where the placid-eyed and lazy-footed cattle came
> to drink,
And the tilting snipe stood fearless of the truant's
> wayward cry
And the splashing of the swimmer, in the days
> gone by.

O the days gone by! O the days gone by!
The music of the laughing lip, the lustre of the eye;
The childish faith in fairies, and Aladdin's magic
> ring—
The simple, soul-reposing, glad belief in every-
> thing,—
When life was like a story holding neither sob nor
> sigh,
In the golden olden glory of the days gone by.

CHRISTMAS AFTERTHOUGHT

AFTER a thoughtful, almost painful pause,
Bub sighed, "I'm sorry fer old *Santy Claus:*—
They *wuz* no Santy Claus, ner *couldn't* be,
When *he* wuz ist a little boy like me!"

THE ROBINS' OTHER NAME

In the Orchard-Days, when you
Children look like blossoms, too;
Bessie, with her jaunty ways
And trim poise of head and face,
Must have looked superior
Even to the blossoms,—for
Little Winnie once averred
Bessie looked just like the bird
Tilted on the topmost spray
Of the apple-boughs in May,
With the red breast, and the strong,
Clear, sweet warble of his song.—
"I don't know their *name*," Win said
"I ist *maked* a name instead."—
So forever afterwards
We called robins "Bessie-birds."

TO HATTIE—ON HER BIRTHDAY

Written in "A Child's Garden of Verses"

WHEN your "Uncle Jim" was younger,
In the days of childish hunger
For the honey of such verses
As this little book rehearses
    In such sweet simplicity,—
Just the simple gift that this is
Would have brimmed his heart with blisses
Sweet as Hattie's sweetest kisses,
    On her anniversary.

THE CHRISTMAS LONG AGO

Come, sing a hale Heigh-ho
For the Christmas long ago!—
When the old log-cabin homed us
    From the night of blinding snow,
When the rarest joy held reign,
And the chimney roared amain,
With the firelight like a beacon
    Through the frosty window-pane.

Ah! the revel and the din
From without and from within,
The blend of distant sleigh-bells
    With the plinking violin;
The muffled shrieks and cries—
Then the glowing cheeks and eyes—
The driving storm of greetings,
    Gusts of kisses and surprise.

THE CHRISTMAS LONG AGO

Sing—sweetest of all glees—
Of the taffy-makers, please,—
And, round the saucers in the snow,
　　The children thick as bees;
　And sing each chubby cheek,
　Chin and laughing lip astreak
With still a sweeter sweetness than
　　The tongue of Song can speak.

　Sing in again the mirth
　Of the circle round the hearth,
With the rustic Sindbad telling us
　　The strangest tales on earth!
　And the Minstrel Bard we knew,
　With his "Love-i-er so True,"
Likewise his "Young House-K-yarpen-*ter*
　　And "Lovèd Henry," too!

　And, forgetting ne'er a thing,
　Lift a gladder voice and sing
Of the dancers in the kitchen—
　　Clean from start to "pigeon-wing"!
　Sing the glory and the glee
　And the joy and jubilee,—

THE CHRISTMAS LONG AGO

The twirling form—the quickened breath—
    The sigh of ecstasy.—

  The eyes that smile alone
  Back into our happy own—
The leaping pulse—the laughing blood—
    The trembling undertone!—
  Ho! pair us off once more,
    With our feet upon the floor
And our heads and hearts in heaven,
    As they were in days of yore!

MABEL

Sweet little face, so full of slumber now—
  Sweet lips uplifted now with any kiss—
Sweet dimpled cheek and chin, and snowy brow,—
      What quietude is this?

O speak! Have you forgotten, yesterday,
  How gladly you came running to the gate
To meet us in the old familiar way,
      So joyous—so elate—

So filled with wildest glee, yet so serene
  With innocence of song and childish chat,
With all the dear caresses in between—
      Have you forgotten that?

Have you forgotten, knowing gentler charms,
  The boisterous love of one you ran to greet
When you last met, who caught you in his arms
      And kissed you, in the street?

MABEL

Not very many days have passed since then,
    And yet between that kiss and him there lies
No pathway of return—unless again,
        In streets of Paradise,

Your eager feet come twinkling down the gold
    Of some bright thoroughfare ethereal,
To meet and greet him there just as of old.—
        Till then, farewell—farewell.

LITTLE GIRLY-GIRL

Little Girly-Girl, of you
   Still forever I am dreaming.-
Laughing eyes of limpid blue—
   Tresses glimmering and gleaming
Like glad waters running over
Shelving shallows, rimmed with clover,
   Trembling where the eddies whirl,
   Gurgling, "Little Girly-Girl!"

For your name it came to me
   Down the brink of brooks that brought it
Out of Paradise—and we—
   Love and I—we, leaning, caught it
From the ripples romping nigh us,
And the bubbles bumping by us
   Over shoals of pebbled pearl,
   Lilting, "Little Girly-Girl!"

LITTLE GIRLY-GIRL

That was long and long ago,
   But in memory the tender
Winds of summer weather blow,
   And the roses burst in splendor;
And the meadow's grassy billows
Break in blossoms round the willows
   Where the currents curve and curl
   Calling, "Little Girly-Girl!"

JACK-IN-THE-BOX

[Grandfather, musing]

In childish days! O memory,
You bring such curious things to me!—
Laughs to the lip—tears to the eye,
In looking on the gifts that lie .
Like broken playthings scattered o'er
Imagination's nursery floor!
Did these old hands once click the key
That let "Jack's" box-lid upward fly,
And that blear-eyed, fur-whiskered elf
Leap, as though frightened at himself,
And quiveringly lean and stare
At me, his jailer, laughing there?

A child then! Now—I only know
They call me very old; and so
They will not let me have my way,—
But uselessly I sit all day

JACK-IN-THE-BOX

Here by the chimney-jamb, and poke
The lazy fire, and smoke and smoke,
And watch the wreaths swoop up the flue,
And chuckle—ay, I often do—
Seeing again, all vividly,
Jack-in-the-box leap, as in glee
To see how much he looks like me!

. . . They talk. I can't hear what they say—
But I am glad, clean through and through
Sometimes, in fancying that they
Are saying, "Sweet, that fancy strays
In age back to our childish days!"

TIME OF CLEARER TWITTERINGS

I

Time of crisp and tawny leaves,
And of tarnished harvest sheaves,
And of dusty grasses—weeds—
Thistles, with their tufted seeds
Voyaging the Autumn breeze
Like as fairy argosies:
Time of quicker flash of wings,
And of clearer twitterings
In the grove or deeper shade
Of the tangled everglade,—
Where the spotted water-snake
Coils him in the sunniest brake;
And the bittern, as in fright,
Darts, in sudden, slanting flight,
Southward, while the startled crane
Films his eyes in dreams again.

TIME OF CLEARER TWITTERINGS

II

Down along the dwindled creek
We go loitering.   We speak
Only with old questionings
Of the dear remembered things
Of the days of long ago,
When the stream seemed thus and so
In our boyish eyes:—The bank
Greener then, through rank on rank
Of the mottled sycamores,
Touching tops across the shores:
Here, the hazel thicket stood—
There, the almost pathless wood
Where the shellbark hickory-tree
Rained its wealth on you and me.
Autumn! as you loved us then,
Take us to your heart again!

III

Season halest of the year!
How the zestful atmosphere
Nettles blood and brain and smites
Into life the old delights

TIME OF CLEARER TWITTERINGS

We have wasted in our youth,
And our graver years, forsooth!
How again the boyish heart
Leaps to see the chipmunk start
From the brush and sleek the sun's
Very beauty, as he runs!
How again a subtle hint
Of crushed pennyroyal or mint
Sends us on our knees, as when
We were truant boys of ten—
Brown marauders of the wood,
Merrier than Robin Hood!

IV

Ah! will any minstrel say,
In his sweetest roundelay,
What is sweeter, after all,
Than black haws, in early Fall?—
Fruit so sweet the frost first sat,
Dainty-toothed, and nibbled at!
And will any poet sing
Of a lusher, richer thing

TIME OF CLEARER TWITTERINGS

Than a ripe May-apple, rolled
Like a pulpy lump of gold
Under thumb and finger-tips,
And poured molten through the lips?
Go, ye bards of classic themes,
Pipe your songs by classic streams!
I would twang the redbird's wings
In the thicket while he sings!

ON THE SUNNY SIDE

Hi and whoop-hooray, boys!
    Sing a song of cheer!
Here's a holiday, boys,
    Lasting half a year!
Round the world, and half is
    Shadow we have tried;
Now we're where the laugh is,—
    On the sunny side!

Pigeons coo and mutter,
    Strutting high aloof
Where the sunbeams flutter
    Through the stable roof.
Hear the chickens cheep, boys,
    And the hen with pride
Clucking them to sleep, boys,
    On the sunny side!

Hear the clacking guinea;
    Hear the cattle moo;
Hear the horses whinny,
    Looking out at you!

ON THE SUNNY SIDE

On the hitching-block, boys,
    Grandly satisfied,
See the old peacock, boys,
    On the sunny side!

Robins in the peach-tree;
    Bluebirds in the pear;
Blossoms over each tree
    In the orchard there!
All the world's in joy, boys,
    Glad and glorified
As a romping boy, boys,
    On the sunny side!

Where's a heart as mellow—
    Where's a soul as free—
Where is any fellow
    We would rather be?
Just ourselves or none, boys,
    World around and wide,
Laughing in the sun, boys,
    On the sunny side!

THE ALL-GOLDEN

I

THROUGH every happy line I sing
I feel the tonic of the Spring.
The day is like an old-time face
That gleams across some grassy place
An old-time face—an old-time chum
Who rises from the grave to come
And lure me back along the ways
Of time's all-golden yesterdays.
Sweet day! to thus remind me of
The truant boy I used to love—
To set, once more, his finger-tips
Against the blossom of his lips,
And pipe for me the signal known
By none but him and me alone!

THE ALL-GOLDEN

II

I see, across the school-room floor,
The shadow of the open door,
And dancing dust and sunshine blent
Slanting the way the morning went,
And beckoning my thoughts afar
Where reeds and running waters are;
Where amber-colored bayous glass
The half-drown'd weeds and wisps of grass.
Where sprawling frogs, in loveless key,
Sing on and on incessantly.
Against the green wood's dim expanse
The cattail tilts its tufted lance,
While on its tip—one might declare
The white "snake-feeder" blossomed there!

III

I catch my breath as children do
In woodland swings when life is new,
And all the blood is warm as wine
And tingles with a tang divine.
My soul soars up the atmosphere
And sings aloud where God can hear,

THE ALL-GOLDEN

And all my being leans intent
To mark His smiling wonderment.
O gracious dream, and gracious time,
And gracious theme, and gracious rhyme—
When buds of Spring begin to blow
In blossoms that we used to know
And lure us back along the ways
Of time's all-golden yesterdays!

LONGFELLOW'S LOVE FOR THE CHILDREN

Awake, he loved their voices,
  And wove them into his rhyme;
And the music of their laughter
  Was with him all the time.

Though he knew the tongues of nations,
  And their meanings all were dear,
The prattle and lisp of a little child
  Was the sweetest for him to hear.

WINTER FANCIES

I

Winter without
    And warmth within;
The winds may shout
    And the storm begin;
The snows may pack
    At the window-pane,
And the skies grow black,
    And the sun remain
Hidden away
    The livelong day—
But here—in here is the warmth of May!

II

Swoop your spitefullest
    Up the flue,
    Wild Winds—do!
What in the world do I care for you?

WINTER FANCIES

    O delightfullest
        Weather of all,
        Howl and squall,
And shake the trees till the last leaves fall!

III

    The joy one feels,
        In an easy-chair,
    Cocking his heels
        In the dancing air
That wreaths the rim of a roaring stove
Whose heat loves better than hearts can love
        Will not permit
           The coldest day
              To drive away
The fire in his blood, and the bliss of it!

IV

    Then blow, Winds, blow!
        And rave and shriek,
    And snarl and snow,
        Till your breath grows weak—

WINTER FANCIES

While here in my room
    I'm as snugly shut
As a glad little worm
    In the heart of a nut!

THE PRAYER PERFECT

Dear Lord! kind Lord!
    Gracious Lord! I pray
Thou wilt look on all I love,
    Tenderly to-day!
Weed their hearts of weariness
    Scatter every care
Down a wake of angel-wings
    Winnowing the air.

Bring unto the sorrowing
    All release from pain;
Let the lips of laughter
    Overflow again;
And with all the needy
    O divide, I pray,
This vast treasure of content
    That is mine to-day!

A MOTHER-SONG

Mother, O mother! forever I cry for you,
  Sing the old song I may never forget;
Even in slumber I murmur and sigh for you.—
  Mother, O Mother,
       Sing low, "Little brother,
Sleep, for thy mother bends over thee yet!"

Mother, O mother! the years are so lonely,
  Filled but with weariness, doubt and regret!
Can't you come back to me—for to-night only,
  Mother, my mother,
       And sing, "Little brother,
Sleep, for thy mother bends over thee yet!"

Mother, O mother! of old I had never
  One wish denied me, nor trouble to fret;
Now—must I cry out all vainly forever,—
  Mother, sweet mother,
       O sing, "Little brother,
Sleep, for thy mother bends over thee yet!"

A MOTHER-SONG

Mother, O mother! must longing and sorrow
  Leave me in darkness, with eyes ever wet,
And never the hope of a meeting to-morrow?
  Answer me, mother,
          And sing, "Little brother,
Sleep, for thy mother bends over thee yet!"

IN THE NIGHT

WHEN it's night, and no light, too,
    Wakin' by yourse'f,
With the old clock mockin' you
    On the mantel-she'f;
In the dark—so still and black,
    You're afeard you'll hear
Somepin' awful pop and crack,—
    "Go to sleep, my dear!"

That's what *Mother* says.—And *ther's*
    When we ain't *afeard!*
Wunder, when we be big mens,
    Then 'ul we be skeerd?—
Some night Mother's goned away,
    And ist *us* is here,
Will The Good Man wake and say,
    "Go to sleep, my dear"?

THE FUNNY LITTLE FELLOW

'Twas a Funny Little Fellow
    Of the very purest type,
For he had a heart as mellow
    As an apple overripe;
And the brightest little twinkle
    When a funny thing occurred,
And the lightest little tinkle
    Of a laugh you ever heard!

His smile was like the glitter
    Of the sun in tropic lands,
And his talk a sweeter twitter,
    Than the swallow understands;
Hear him sing—and tell a story—
    Snap a joke—ignite a pun,—
'Twas a capture—rapture—glory,
    And explosion—all in one!

THE FUNNY LITTLE FELLOW

Though he hadn't any money—
    That condiment which tends
To make a fellow "honey"
    For the palate of his friends;—
Sweet simples he compounded—
    Sovereign antidotes for sin
Or taint,—a faith unbounded
    That his friends were genuine.

He wasn't honored, maybe—
    For his songs of praise were slim,—
Yet I never knew a baby
    That wouldn't crow for him;
I never knew a mother
    But urged a kindly claim
Upon him as a brother,
    At the mention of his name.

The sick have ceased their sighing,
    And have even found the grace
Of a smile when they were dying
    As they looked upon his face;

THE FUNNY LITTLE FELLOW

And I've seen his eyes of laughter
    Melt in tears that only ran
As though, swift-dancing after,
    Came the Funny Little Man.

He laughed away the sorrow
    And he laughed away the gloom
We are all so prone to borrow
    From the darkness of the tomb;
And he laughed across the ocean
    Of a happy life, and passed,
With a laugh of glad emotion,
    Into Paradise at last.

And I think the Angels knew him,
    And had gathered to await
His coming, and run to him
    Through the widely opened Gate
With their faces gleaming sunny
    For his laughter-loving sake,
And thinking, "What a funny
    Little Angel he will make!"

UNCLE SIDNEY'S VIEWS

I HOLD that the true age of wisdom is when
We are boys and girls, and not women and men,—
When as credulous children we *know* things because
We *believe* them—however averse to the laws.
It is *faith*, then, not science and reason, I say,
That is genuine wisdom.—And would that to-day
We, as then, were as wise and ineffably blest
As to live, love and die, and trust God for the rest!

So I simply deny the old notion, you know,
That the wiser we get as the older we grow!—
For *in youth* all we know we are *certain* of.—*Now*
The greater our knowledge, the more we allow
For sceptical margin.—And hence I regret
That the world isn't flat, and the sun doesn't set,
And we may not go creeping up home, when we
    die,
Through the moon, like a round yellow hole in the
    sky.

WHEN EARLY MARCH SEEMS MIDDLE MAY

When country roads begin to thaw
   In mottled spots of damp and dust,
And fences by the margin draw
     Along the frosty crust
   Their graphic silhouettes, I say,
   The Spring is coming round this way.

When morning-time is bright with sun
   And keen with wind, and both confuse
The dancing, glancing eyes of one
     With tears that ooze and ooze—
   And nose-tips weep as well as they,
   The Spring is coming round this way.

When suddenly some shadow-bird
   Goes wavering beneath the gaze,
And through the hedge the moan is heard
     Of kine that fain would graze
   In grasses new, I smile and say,
   The Spring is coming round this way.

WHEN EARLY MARCH SEEMS MIDDLE MAY

When knotted horse-tails are untied,
   And teamsters whistle here and there,
And clumsy mitts are laid aside
     And choppers' hands are bare,
   And chips are thick where children play,
   The Spring is coming round this way.

When through the twigs the farmer tramps,
   And troughs are chunked beneath the trees,
And fragrant hints of sugar-camps
     Astray in every breeze,—
   When early March seems middle May,
   The Spring is coming round this way.

When coughs are changed to laughs, and when
   Our frowns melt into smiles of glee,
And all our blood thaws out again
     In streams of ecstasy,
   And poets wreak their roundelay,
   The Spring is coming round this way.

THE NINE LITTLE GOBLINS

They all climbed up on a high board-fence—
  Nine little goblins, with green-glass eyes—
Nine little goblins that had no sense,
    And couldn't tell coppers from cold mince-pies;
      And they all climbed up on the fence, and sat—
      And I asked them what they were staring at.

And the first one said, as he scratched his head
  With a queer little arm that reached out of his ear
And rasped its claws in his hair so red—
    "This is what this little arm is fer!"
      And he scratched and stared, and the next one said,
      "How on earth do *you* scratch your head?"

And he laughed like the screech of a rusty hinge—
  Laughed and laughed till his face grew black;
And when he choked, with a final twinge
    Of his stifling laughter, he thumped his back

THE NINE LITTLE GOBLINS

    With a fist that grew on the end of his tail
    Till the breath came back to his lips so pale.

And the third little goblin leered round at me—
  And there were no lids on his eyes at all,—
And he clucked one eye, and he says, says he,
  "What is the style of your socks this fall?"
    And he clapped his heels—and I sighed to see
    That he had hands where his feet should be.

Then a bald-faced goblin, gray and grim,
  Bowed his head, and I saw him slip
His eyebrows off, as I looked at him,
  And paste them over his upper lip;
    And then he moaned in remorseful pain—
    "Would—Ah, would I'd me brows again!"

And then the whole of the goblin band
  Rocked on the fence-top to and fro,
And clung, in a long row, hand in hand,
  Singing the songs that they used to know—
    Singing the songs that their grandsires sung
    In the goo-goo days of the goblin-tongue.

THE NINE LITTLE GOBLINS

And ever they kept their green-glass eyes
  Fixed on me with a stony stare—
Till my own grew glazed with a dread surmise,
  And my hat whooped up on my lifted hair,
    And I felt the heart in my breast snap to,
    As you've heard the lid of a snuff-box do.

And they sang: "You're asleep! There is no board-fence,
  And never a goblin with green-glass eyes!—
'Tis only a vision the mind invents
  After a supper of cold mince-pies.—
    And you're doomed to dream this way," they said,—
    "*And you sha'n't wake up till you're clean plum dead!*"

THE LITTLE COAT

HERE's his ragged "roundabout." .
Turn the pockets inside out:
See; his penknife, lost to use,
Rusted shut with apple-juice;
Here, with marbles, top and string,
Is his deadly "devil-sling,"
With its rubber, limp at last
As the sparrows of the past!
Beeswax—buckles—leather straps—
Bullets, and a box of caps,—
Not a thing of all, I guess,
But betrays some waywardness—
E'en these tickets, blue and red,
For the Bible-verses said—
Such as this his mem'ry kept,—
            "Jesus wept."

THE LITTLE COAT

Here's a fishing-hook and -line,
Tangled up with wire and twine,
And dead angleworms, and some
Slugs of lead and chewing-gum,
Blent with scents that can but come
From the oil of rhodium.
Here—a soiled, yet dainty note,
That some little sweetheart wrote,
Dotting—"Vine grows round the stump
And—"My sweetest sugar-lump!"
Wrapped in this—a padlock key
Where he's filed a touch-hole—see!
And some powder in a quill
Corked up with a liver pill;
And a spongy little chunk
           Of "punk."

Here's the little coat—but O
Where is he we've censured so?
Don't you hear us calling, dear?
Back! come back, and never fear.—
You may wander where you will,
Over orchard, field and hill;

THE LITTLE COAT

You may kill the birds, or do
Anything that pleases you!
Ah, this empty coat of his!
Every tatter worth a kiss;
Every stain as pure instead
As the white stars overhead:
And the pockets—homes were they
Of the little hands that play
Now no more—but, absent, thus
                  Beckon us.

LAWYER AND CHILD

How large was Alexander, father,
    That parties designate
The historic gentleman as rather
    Inordinately great?

Why, son, to speak with conscientious
    Regard for history,
Waiving all claims, of course, to heights
      pretentious,—
    About the size of me.

EXCEEDING ALL

Long life's a lovely thing to know,
  With lovely health and wealth, forsooth
And lovely name and fame—But O
      The loveliness of Youth!

THE DREAM OF THE LITTLE PRINCESS

'Twas a curious dream, good sooth!—
    The dream of The Little Princess;
It seemed a dream, yet a truth,
Long years ago in her youth.—
    It *came* as a dream—no less
    It was *not* a dream, she says.

(She is singing and saying things
    Musical as the wile
Of the eerie quaverings
That drip from the grievèd strings
    Of her lute.—We weep or smile
    Even as she, meanwhile.)

THE DREAM OF THE LITTLE PRINCESS

In a day, long dead and gone,
    When her castle-turrets threw
Their long, sharp shadows on
The sward like lances,—wan
    And lone, she strayed into
    Strange grounds where lilies grew.

There, late in the afternoon,
    As she sate in the terrace shade,
Rav'ling a half-spun tune
From a lute like a wee new-moon,—
    High off was a bugle played,
    And a sound as of steeds that neighed

And the lute fell from her hands,
    As her eyes raised, half in doubt,
To the arch of the azure lands
Where lo! with the fluttering strands
    Of a rainbow reined about
    His wrist, rode a horseman out.

And The Little Princess was stirred
    No less at his steeds than him;—

THE DREAM OF THE LITTLE PRINCESS

A jet-black span of them gird
In advance, he bestrode the third;
    And the troop of them seemed to swim
    The skies as the Seraphim.

Wingless they were, yet so
    Upborne in their wondrous flight—
As their master bade them go,
They dwindled on high; or lo!
    They curved from their heavenmost height
    And swooped to her level sight.

And the eyes of The Little Princess
    Grow O so bright as the chants
Of the horseman's courtliness,—
Saluting her low—Ah, yes!
    And lifting a voice that haunts
    Her own song's weird romance.

For (she sings) at last he swept
    As near to her as the tips
Of the lilies, that whitely slept,
As he leaned o'er one and wept
    And touched it with his lips—
    Sweeter than honey-drips!

THE DREAM OF THE LITTLE PRINCESS

And she keeps the lily yet—
    As the horseman bade (she says)
As he launched, with a wild curvet,
His steeds toward the far sunset,
    Till gulfed in its gorgeousness
    And lost to The Little Princess:

But O, my master sweet!
    He is coming again! (*she sings*)
My Prince of the Coursers fleet,
    With his bugle's echoings,
    And the breath of his voice for the wings
Of the sandals of his feet!

THE LAND OF USED-TO-BE

AND where's the Land of Used-to-be, does little
    baby wonder?
  Oh, we will clap a magic saddle over "Poppie's"
    knee
And ride away around the world, and in and out
    and under
  The whole of all the golden sunny Summer-
    time and see.

Leisurely and lazy-like we'll jostle on our journey,
  And let the pony bathe his hooves and cool them
    in the dew,
As he sidles down the shady way, and lags along
    the ferny
  And green, grassy edges of the lane we travel
    through.

And then we'll canter on to catch the bubble of the
    thistle
  As it bumps among the butterflies and glimmers
    down the sun,

THE LAND OF USED-TO-BE

To leave us laughing, all content to hear the robin
    whistle
  Or guess what Katydid is saying little Katy's
    done.

And pausing here a minute, where we hear the
    squirrel chuckle
  As he darts from out the underbrush and scam-
    pers up the tree,
We will gather buds and locust-blossoms, leaves
    and honeysuckle,
  To wreathe around our foreheads, riding into
    Used-to-be;—

For here's the very rim of it that we go swinging
    over—
  Don't you hear the Fairy bugles, and the tinkle
    of the bells,
And see the baby-bumblebees that tumble in the
    clover
  And dangle from the tilted pinks and tipsy pim-
    pernels?

And don't you see the merry faces of the daffo-
          dillies,
   And the jolly Johnny-jump-ups, and the butter-
          cups a-glee,
And the low, lolling ripples ring around the water-
          lilies?—
   All greeting us with laughter, to the Land of
          Used-to-be!

And here among the blossoms of the blooming
          vines and grasses,
   With a haze forever hanging in the sky forever
          blue,
And with a breeze from over seas to kiss us as it
          passes,
   We will romp around forever as the airy Elfins
          do!

For all the elves of earth and air are swarming
          here together—
   The prankish Puck, King Oberon, and Queen
          Titania too;
And dear old Mother Goose herself, as sunny as
          the weather,
   Comes dancing down the dewy walks to wel-
          come me and you!

WHEN OUR BABY DIED

Wʜᴇɴ our baby died—
My Ma she ist cried an' cried!
Yes 'n' my Pa *he* cried, too—
An' *I* cried—An' me an' you.—
An' I 'tended like my doll
She cried too—An' ever'—all—
O ist *ever'body* cried
　　When our baby died!

When our baby died—
Nen I got to took a ride!
An' we all ist rode an' rode
Clean to Heav'n where baby goed—
Mighty nigh!—An' nen Ma she
Cried ag'in—an' Pa—an' me.—
All but ist the *Angels* cried
　　When our baby died!

CHRISTINE BRAIBRY

THE BEAUTIFUL DOLLY WHO COMES FROM TENTOLEENA LAND BRINGING A STRANGE LETTER

The Letter

This little Dolly's name is Christine Braibry.* She was born in Tentoleena Land, where lilies and red roses grow in the air, and humming-birds and butterflies on stalks.

You must be kind to Christine, for everything about her in your land will be very strange to her. If she seems to stare in a bewildered way, and will not answer when you ask her why, you must know that she is simply dazed with the wonders that she sees on every hand. It will doubtless be a long, long while before Christine will cease to marvel at the Sunshine of your strange country; for in Ten-

* The terminal of this name is sounded short, as in "lovely."

CHRISTINE BRAIBRY

toleena Land there is never any shine but Moonshine, and sometimes that gets so muddied up with shade it soils the eyesight to gaze at it overmuch.

It will be trying, in your land, for Christine to keep silent all the time, for, in your country, Dollies cannot walk and talk at all perfectly, because they only think they are dreaming all the time, and they dare not speak for fear their voices will awaken them, and they dare not move for fear of falling out of bed. So, you see, you should be very kind indeed to little Christine Braibry.

In Tentoleena Land the Dollies do not sleep long—they are always the first ones up at Moon-dawn—for Moon-dawn is the Dollies' morning. Then they go out in the fragrant grasses, where the big, ripe dewdrops grow—much nicer, purer dew than yours on earth, for in Tentoleena Land they gather it before it has been skimmed, and all the pearly cream that gathers on the surface of the drops they stir up with the rest and bathe in that; and this is why the Dollies always have such delicate complexions. Then, when the baths are over, they dress themselves, and waken their parents.

and dress them—for in Tentoleena Land the parents are the children. Is not that odd?

Sometime Christine may get used to your strange land and all the wonders that she sees; and if she ever does, and smiles at you, and pulls your face down close to hers and kisses you, why, that will be the sign by which you'll know she's coming to again and wants to talk; and so the first thing you must ask of her is to sing this little song she made of Tentoleena Land. Only the words of it can be given here—(not half the beauty of the dainty song)—for when you *hear* it, in the marvellously faint, and low, and sweet, and tender, tinkling tongue of Tentoleena Land, you will indeed be glad that the gracious fairy Fortune ever sent you Christine Braibry.

So, since all the sounds in the melodious utterance of Tentoleena Land are so exquisitely, so chastely, rarely beautiful no earthly art may hope to reproduce them, you must, as you here read the words, just shut your eyes and *fancy* that you hear little Christine Braibry singing this eerie song of hers:—

CHRISTINE'S SONG

Up in Tentoleena Land—
    Tentoleena! Tentoleena!
All the Dollies, hand in hand,
    Mina, Nainie, and Serena,
Dance the Fairy fancy dances,
With glad songs and starry glances,
Lisping roundelays; and, after,
Bird-like interludes of laughter
Strewn and scattered o'er the lawn
Their gilt sandals twinkle on
Through light mists of silver sand
    Up in Tentoleena Land.

Up in Tentoleena Land—
    Tentoleena! Tentoleena!
Blares the eerie Elfin band—
    Trumpet, harp and concertina
Larkspur bugle—honeysuckle
Cornet, with a quickstep chuckle
In its golden throat; and, maybe,
Lilies-of-the-valley they be

CHRISTINE BRAIBRY

Baby-silver-bells that chime
Musically all the time,
Tossed about from hand to hand—
    Up in Tentoleena Land.

Up in Tentoleena Land—
    Tentoleena! Tentoleena!
Dollies dark, and blonde and bland—
    Sweet as musk-rose or verbena-
Sweet as moon-blown daffodillies,
    Or wave-jostled water-lilies,
Yearning to'rd the rose-mouths, ready
Leaning o'er the river's eddy,—
Dance, and glancing fling to you,
Through these lines you listen to,
Kisses blown from lip and hand
    Out of Tentoleena Land!

THE SQUIRT-GUN UNCLE MAKED ME

Uncle Sidney, when he was here,
    Maked me a squirt-gun out o' some
Elder-bushes 'at growed out near
Where wuz the brick-yard—'way out clear
        To where the Toll Gate come!

So when we walked back home again,
    He maked it, out in our woodhouse where
Wuz the old work-bench, an' the old jack-plane,
An' the old 'poke-shave, an' the tools all lay'n'
        Ist like he wants 'em there.

He sawed it first with the old hand-saw;
    An' nen he peeled off the bark, an' got
Some glass an' scraped it; an' told 'bout Pa,
When *he* wuz a boy an' fooled his Ma,
        An' the whippin' 'at he caught.

THE SQUIRT-GUN UNCLE MAKED ME

Nen Uncle Sidney, he took an' filed
    A' old arn ramrod; an' one o' the ends
He screwed fast into the vise; an' smiled,
Thinkin', he said, o' when he wuz a child,
        'Fore him an' Pa wuz mens.

He punched out the peth, an' nen he putt
    A plug in the end with a hole notched through
Nen took the old drawey-knife an' cut
An' maked a handle 'at shoved clean shut
        But ist where yer hand held to.

An' he wropt th'uther end with some string an
    white
    Piece o' the sleeve of a' old tored shirt;
An' nen he showed me to hold it tight,
An' suck in the water an' work it right.—
        An' it 'ud ist squirt an' squirt!

THE BROOK-SONG

LITTLE brook! Little brook!
You have such a happy look—
Such a very merry manner, as you swerve and
        curve and crook—
And your ripples, one and one,
Reach each other's hands and run
   Like laughing little children in the sun!

Little brook, sing to me:
Sing about a bumblebee
That tumbled from a lily-bell and grumbled mum-
        blingly,
Because he wet the film
Of his wings, and had to swim,
   While the water-bugs raced round and
   laughed at him!

THE BROOK-SONG

Little brook—sing a song
Of a leaf that sailed along
Down the golden-braided centre of your current
swift and strong,
And a dragon-fly that lit
On the tilting rim of it,
And rode away and wasn't scared a bit.

And sing—how oft in glee
Came a truant boy like me,
Who loved to lean and listen to your lilting melody,
Till the gurgle and refrain
Of your music in his brain
Wrought a happiness as keen to him as
pain.

Little brook—laugh and leap!
Do not let the dreamer weep:
Sing him all the songs of summer till he sink in
softest sleep;
And then sing soft and low
Through his dreams of long ago—
Sing back to him the rest he used to know!

THE YOUTHFUL PRESS.

Little Georgie Tompers, he
Printed some fine cards for me;
But his press had "J" for *James*—
By no means the choice of names.—

Yet it's proper, none the less,
That his little printing-press
Should be taught that *James* for "J"
Always is the better way.

For, if left to its own whim,
Next time it might call me "Jim,"—
Then The Cultured Press would be
Shocked at such a liberty.

Therefore, little presses all
Should be trained, while they are small
To develop *taste* in these
Truths that shape our destinies.

THAT-AIR YOUNG-UN

That-air young-un ust to set
By the crick here day by day,—
Watch the swallers dip and wet
Their slim wings and skoot away;
Watch these little snipes along
The low banks tilt up and down
'Mongst the reeds, and hear the song
Of the bullfrogs croakin' roun':
Ust to set here in the sun
Watchin' things, and listenun,
'Peared-like, mostly to the roar
Of the dam below, er to
That-air riffle nigh the shore
Jes acrost from me and you.
Ust to watch him from the door
Of the mill.—Ud rigg him out
With a fishin'-pole and line—
Dig worms fer him—nigh about

THAT-AIR YOUNG-UN

Jes spit on his bait!—but he
Never keered much, 'pearantly,
To ketch fish!—He 'druther fine
Out some sunny place, and set
Watchin' things, with droopy head,
And "a-listenun," he said—
"Kindo' listenun above
The old crick to what the wet
Warter was a-talkin' of!"

Jevver hear sich talk as that?
Bothered *Mother* more'n me
What the child was cipher'n' at.—
Come home onc't and said 'at he
Knowed what the snake-feeders thought
When they grit their wings; and knowed
Turkle-talk, when bubbles riz
Over where the old roots growed
Where he th'owed them pets o' his—
Little turripuns he caught
In the County Ditch and packed
In his pockets days and days!—
Said he knowed what goslin's quacked—
Could tell what the killdees sayes,

THAT-AIR YOUNG-UN

And grasshoppers, when they lit
In the crick and "minnies" bit
Off their legs.—"But, *blame!*" says he
Sorto' lookin' clean above
Mother's head and on through me—
(And them eyes!—I see 'em yet!)—
"*Blame!*" he says, "ef I kin see,
Er make *out*, jes what the wet
Warter is a-talkin' of!"

Made me *nervous!* Mother, though,
Said best not to scold the child—
The Good Bein' knowed.—And so
We was only rickonciled
When he'd be asleep.—And then,
Time, and time, and time again,
We've watched over him, you know—
Her a-sayin' nothin'—jes
Kindo' smoothin' back his hair,
And, all to herse'f, I guess,
Studyin' up some kind o' prayer
She ain't tried yet.—Onc't she said,
Cotin' Scriptur', "'He,'" says she,
In a solemn whisper, "'He
Givuth His beloved sleep!'"

THAT-AIR YOUNG-UN

And jes then I heerd the rain
Strike the shingles, as I turned
Res'less to'rds the wall again.
Pity strong men dast to weep!—
Specially when up above
Thrash! the storm comes down and you
Feel the midnight plum soaked through
Heart and soul, and wunder, too,
What the warter's talkin' of!

. . . . .

Found his hat 'way down below
Hinchman's Ford.—'Ves' Anders he
Rid and fetched it. Mother she
Went *wild* over that, you know—
Hugged it! kissed it!—*Turribul!*
My hopes then was all gone too. . . .
Brung him in, with both hands full
O' warter-lilies—'peared-like new-
Bloomed fer him—renched whiter still
In the clear rain, mixin' fine
And finer in the noon sunshine. . . .

THAT-AIR YOUNG-UN

Winders of the old mill looked
On him where the hill-road crooked
In on through the open gate. . . .
Laid him on the old settee
On the porch there.   Heerd the great
Roarin' dam acrost—and we
Heerd a crane cry in amongst
The sycamores—and then a dove
Cutterin' on the mill-roof—then
Heerd the crick, and thought again,
"*Now* what's it a-talkin' of?"

BABY'S DYING

Baby's dying,
    Do not stir—
        Let her spirit lightly float
Through the sighing
    Lips of her—
        Still the murmur in the throat
    Let the moan of grief be curbed—
Baby must not be disturbed!

Baby's dying,
    Do not stir—
        Let her pure life lightly swim
Through the sighing
    Lips of her—
        Out from us and up to HIM—
Let her leave us with that smile—
    Kiss and miss her after while.

THE BOYS

Where are they?—the friends of my childhood
    enchanted—
  The clear, laughing eyes looking back in my own,
And the warm, chubby fingers my palms have so
    wanted,
  As when we raced over
            Pink pastures of clover,
And mocked the quail's whir and the bumblebee's
    drone?

Have the breezes of time blown their blossomy
    faces
  Forever adrift down the years that are flown?
Am I never to see them romp back to their places,
  Where over the meadow,
            In sunshine and shadow,
The meadow-larks trill, and the bumblebees drone?

THE BOYS

Where are they? Ah! dim in the dust lies the
    clover;
  The whippoorwill's call has a sorrowful tone,
And the dove's—I have wept at it over and over;—
  I want the glad lustre
        Of youth, and the cluster
Of faces asleep where the bumblebees drone!

OLD MAN'S NURSERY RHYME

I

In the jolly winters
  Of the long-ago,
It was not so cold as now—
  O! No! No!
Then, as I remember,
  Snowballs to eat
Were as good as apples now,
  And every bit as sweet!

II

In the jolly winters
  Of the dead-and-gone,
Bub was warm as summer,
  With his red mitts on,—

OLD MAN'S NURSERY RHYME

Just in his little waist-
   And-pants all together,
Who ever heard him growl
   About cold weather?

III

In the jolly winters
   Of the long-ago—
Was it *half* so cold as now?
   O! No! No!
Who caught his death o' cold,
   Making prints of men
Flat-backed in snow that now's
   Twice as cold again?

IV

In the jolly winters
   Of the dead-and-gone,
Startin' out rabbit huntin'—
   Early as the dawn,—

OLD MAN'S NURSERY RHYME

Who ever froze his fingers,
   Ears, heels, or toes,—
Or'd 'a' cared if he had?
   Nobody knows!

V

Nights by the kitchen-stove,
   Shellin' white and red
Corn in the skillet, and
   Sleepin' four abed!
Ah! the jolly winters
   Of the long-ago!
We were not as old as now—
   O! No! No!

THE SONG OF YESTERDAY

I

But yesterday
I looked away
O'er happy lands, where sunshine lay
In golden blots
Inlaid with spots
Of shade and wild forget-me-nots.

My head was fair
With flaxen hair,
And fragrant breezes, faint and rare,
And, warm with drouth
From out the south,
Blew all my curls across my mouth.

And, cool and sweet,
My naked feet
Found dewy pathways through the wheat
And out again
Where, down the lane,
The dust was dimpled with the rain.

THE SONG OF YESTERDAY

II

But yesterday!—
Adream, astray,
From morning's red to evening's gray
O'er dales and hills
Of daffodills
And lorn sweet-fluting whippoorwills.

I knew nor cares
Nor tears nor prayers—
A mortal god, crowned unawares
With sunset—and
A sceptre-wand
Of apple blossoms in my hand!

The dewy blue
Of twilight grew
To purple, with a star or two
Whose lisping rays
Failed in the blaze
Of sudden fireflies through the haze.

THE SONG OF YESTERDAY

III

But yesterday
I heard the lay
O summer birds, when I, as they
With breast and wing,
All quivering
With life and love, could only sing

My head was lent
Where, with it, blent
A maiden's o'er her instrument;
While all the night,
From vale to height,
Was filled with echoes of delight.

And all our dreams
Were lit with gleams
Of that lost land of reedy streams,
Along whose brim
Forever swim
Pan's lilies, laughing up at him.

THE SONG OF YESTERDAY

IV

But yesterday! . . .
O blooms of May,
And summer roses—where away?
O stars above;
And lips of love,
And all the honeyed sweets thereof!—

O lad and lass,
And orchard pass,
And briered lane, and daisied grass!
O gleam and gloom,
And woodland bloom,
And breezy breaths of all perfume!—

No more for me
Or mine shall be
Thy raptures—save in memory,—
No more—no more—
Till through the Door
Of Glory gleam the days of yore.

DUSK-SONG—THE BEETLE

THE shrilling locust slowly sheathes
   His dagger-voice, and creeps away
Beneath the brooding leaves where breathes
   The zephyr of the dying day:
One naked star has waded through
   The purple shallows of the night,
And faltering as falls the dew
   It drips its misty light.

*   O'er garden blooms,*
*   On tides of musk,*
*   The beetle booms adown the glooms*
*   And bumps along the dusk.*

The katydid is rasping at
   The silence from the tangled broom:
On drunken wings the flitting bat
   Goes staggering athwart the gloom;

DUSK-SONG—THE BEETLE

The toadstool bulges through the weeds
   And lavishly to left and right
The fireflies, like golden seeds,
   Are sown about the night.

   O'er slumbrous blooms,
     On floods of musk,
   The beetle booms adown the glooms
     And bumps along the dusk.

The primrose flares its baby-hands
   Wide open, as the empty moon,
Slow lifted from the underlands,
   Drifts up the azure-arched lagoon;
The shadows on the garden walk
   Are frayed with rifts of silver light;
And, trickling down the poppy-stalk,
   The dewdrop streaks the night.

   O'er folded blooms,
     On swirls of musk,
   The beetle booms adown the glooms
     And bumps along the dusk.

BABYHOOD

Heigh-ho! Babyhood! Tell me where you linger!
  Let's toddle home again, for we have gone astray;
Take this eager hand of mine and lead me by the finger
  Back to the lotus-lands of the far-away!

Turn back the leaves of life.—Don't read the story.—
  Let's find the pictures, and fancy all the rest;
We can fill the written pages with a brighter glory
  Than old Time, the story-teller, at his very best.

Turn to the brook where the honeysuckle tipping
  O'er its vase of perfume spills it on the breeze,
And the bee and humming-bird in ecstasy are sipping
  From the fairy-flagons of the blooming locust-trees.

BABYHOOD

Turn to the lane where we used to "teeter-totter,"
   Printing little foot-palms in the mellow mould—
Laughing at the lazy cattle wading in the water
   Where the ripples dimple round the buttercups of gold.

Where the dusky turtle lies basking on the gravel
   Of the sunny sand-bar in the middle tide,
And the ghostly dragon-fly pauses in his travel
   To rest like a blossom where the water-lily died.

Heigh-ho! Babyhood! Tell me where you linger!
   Let's toddle home again, for we have gone astray;
Take this eager hand of mine and lead me by the finger
   Back to the lotus-lands of the far-away!

MAX AND JIM

Max an' Jim,
    They're each other's
Fat an' slim
    Little brothers.

Max is thin,
    An' Jim, the fac's is,
Fat ag'in
    As little Max is!

Their Pa 'lowed
    He don't know whuther
He's most proud
    Of one er th'other!

Their Ma says
    They're both so sweet—*'m!*—
That she guess
    She'll haf to eat 'em!

THE CIRCUS-DAY PARADE

OH! the Circus-Day Parade! How the bugles
    played and played!
Aud how the glossy horses tossed their flossy manes
    and neighed,
As the rattle and the rhyme of the tenor-drum-
    mer's time
Filled all the hungry hearts of us with melody
    sublime!

How the grand band-wagon shone with a splendor
    all its own,
And glittered with a glory that our dreams had
    never known!
And how the boys behind, high and low of every
    kind,
Marched in unconscious capture, with a rapture
    undefined!

THE CIRCUS-DAY PARADE

How the horsemen, two and two, with their plumes
of white and blue
And crimson, gold and purple, nodding by at me
and you,
Waved the banners that they bore, as the knights
in days of yore,
Till our glad eyes gleamed and glistened like the
spangles that they wore!

How the graceless-graceful stride of the elephant
was eyed,
And the capers of the little horse that cantered at
his side!
How the shambling camels, tame to the plaudits
of their fame,
With listless eyes came silent, masticating as they
came.

How the cages jolted past, with each wagon battened fast,
And the mystery within it only hinted of at last
From the little grated square in the rear, and
nosing there
The snout of some strange animal that sniffed the
outer air!

THE CIRCUS-DAY PARADE

And, last of all, The Clown, making mirth for all
    the town,
With his lips curved ever upward and his eye-
    brows ever down,
And his chief attention paid to the little mule that
    played
A tattoo on the dash-board with his heels, in the
    Parade.

Oh! the Circus-Day Parade! How the bugles
    played and played!
And how the glossy horses tossed their flossy
    manes and neighed,
As the rattle and the rhyme of the tenor-drum-
    mer's time
Filled all the hungry hearts of us with melody sub-
    lime!

THE OLD HAY-MOW

The Old Hay-mow's the place to play
Fer boys, when it's a rainy day!
I good 'eal ruther be up there
Than down in town, er anywhere!

When I play in our stable-loft,
The good old hay's so dry an' soft,
An' feels so fine, an' smells so sweet,
I 'most ferget to go an' eat.

An' one time onc't I *did* ferget
To go tel dinner was all et,—
An' they had short-cake—an'—Bud he
Hogged up the piece Ma saved fer me!

Nen I won't let him play no more
In our hay-mow where I keep store
An' got hen-eggs to sell,—an' shoo
The cackle-un old hen out, too!

THE OLD HAY-MOW

An' nen, when Aunty she was here
A-visitun from Rensselaer,
An' bringed my little cousin,—*he*
Can come up there an' play with me

But, after while—when Bud he bets
'At I can't turn no summersetts,
I let him come up, ef he can
Ac' ha'f-way like a gentleman!

JOHN TARKINGTON JAMESON

John Jameson, my jo John!
  Ye're bonnie wee an' sma';
Your ee's the morning violet,
  Wi' tremblin' dew an' a';
Your smile's the gowden simmer-sheen,
  Wi' glintin' pearls aglow
Atween the posies o' your lips,
  John Jameson, my jo!

Ye hae the faither's braith o' brow,
  An' synes his look benign
Whiles he hings musin' ower the burn,
  Wi' leestless hook an' line;
Ye hae the mither's mou' an' cheek
  An' denty chin—but O!
It's maist ye're like your ain braw sel',
  John Jameson, my jo!

JOHN TARKINGTON JAMESON

John Jameson, my jo John,
   Though, wi' sic luvers twain,
Ye dance far yont your whustlin' frien
   Wha laggart walks his lane,—
Be mindet, though he naps his last
   Whaur kirkyird thistles grow,
His ghaist shall caper on wi' you,
   John Jameson, my jo!

GUINEY-PIGS

Guiney-pigs is awful cute,
With their little trimbly snoot
Sniffin' at the pussly that
We bring 'em to nibble at.
   Looks like they're so clean an' white
   An' so dainty an' polite,
     They could eat like you an' me
       When they's company!

Tiltin' down the clover-tops
Till they spill, an' over drops
The sweet morning dew—Don't you
Think they might have napkins, too?
   Ef a guiney-pig was big
   As a *shore-an'-certain* pig,
     Nen he wouldn't ac' so fine
       When he come to dine.

GUINEY-PIGS

Nen he'd chomp his jaws an' eat
Things out in the dirty street,
Dirt an' all! An' nen lay down
In mud-holes an' waller roun'!
  So the *guiney-pigs* is best,
  'Cause they're nice an' tidiest;
  They eat 'most like you an' me
    When they's company!

BUSCH AND TOMMY

LITTLE Busch and Tommy Hays—
Small the theme, but large the praise,
  For two braver brothers,
Of such toddling years and size,
Bloom of face, and blue of eyes,
Never trampled soldier-wise
  On the rights of mothers!

Even boldly facing their
Therapeutic father's air
  Of complex abstraction,
But to kindle—kindlier gaze,
Wake more smiles and gracious ways
Ay, nor find in all their days
  Ampler satisfaction!

Hail ye, then, with chirp and cheer,
All wan patients, waiting here
  Bitterer medications!
Busch and Tommy, *tone* us, too.—
How our life-blood leaps anew,
Under loving touch of you
  And your ministrations!

HIS CHRISTMAS SLED

I

I watch him, with his Christmas sled
    He hitches on behind
A passing sleigh, with glad hooray,
    And whistles down the wind;
He hears the horses champ their bits,
    And bells that jingle-jingle—
You Woolly Cap! you Scarlet Mitts!
    You miniature "Kriss Kringle!"

I almost catch your secret joy—
    Your chucklings of delight,
The while you whiz where glory is
    Eternally in sight!
With you I catch my breath, as swift
    Your jaunty sled goes gliding
O'er glassy track and shallow drift,
    As I behind were riding!

HIS CHRISTMAS SLED

II

He winks at twinklings of the frost,
  And on his airy race,
Its tingles beat to redder heat
  The rapture of his face:—
The colder, keener is the air,
  The less he cares a feather.
But, there! he's gone! and I gaze on
  The wintriest of weather!

Ah, Boy! still speeding o'er the track
  Where none returns again,
To sigh for you, or cry for you,
  Or die for you were vain.—
And so, speed on! the while I pray
  All nipping frosts forsake you—
Ride still ahead of grief, but may
  All glad things overtake you!

BABE HERRICK

As a rosebud might, in dreams,
'Mid some lilies lie, meseems
Thou, pink youngling, on the breast
Of thy mother slumberest.

THE LAND OF THUS-AND-SO

"How would Willie like to go
To the Land of Thus-and-So?
Everything is proper there—
All the children comb their hair
Smoother than the fur of cats,
Or the nap of high silk hats;
Every face is clean and white
As a lily washed in light;
Never vaguest soil or speck
Found on forehead, throat or neck
Every little crimpled ear,
In and out, as pure and clear
As the cherry-blossom's blow
In the Land of Thus-and-So.

"Little boys that never fall
Down the stair, or cry at all—
Doing nothing to repent,
Watchful and obedient;

THE LAND OF THUS-AND-SO

Never hungry, nor in haste—
Tidy shoe-strings always laced;
Never button rudely torn
From its fellows all unworn;
Knickerbockers always new—
Ribbon, tie, and collar, too;
Little watches, worn like men,
Always promptly half-past ten—
Just precisely right, you know,
For the Land of Thus-and-So!

"And the little babies there
Give no one the slightest care—
Nurse has not a thing to do
But be happy and sigh 'Boo!'
While Mamma just nods, and knows
Nothing but to doze and doze:
Never litter round the grate;
Never lunch or dinner late;
Never any household din
Peals without or rings within—
Baby coos nor laughing calls
On the stairs or through the halls—
Just Great Hushes to and fro
Pace the Land of Thus-and-So!

THE LAND OF THUS-AND-SO

"Oh! the Land of Thus-and-So!—
Isn't it delightful, though?"
"Yes," lisped Willie, answering me
Somewhat slow and doubtfully—
"Must be awful nice, but I
Ruther wait till by and by
'Fore I go there—maybe when
I be dead I'll go there *then*.—
But"—the troubled little face
Closer pressed in my embrace—
"Le's don't never *ever* go
To the Land of Thus-and-So!"

GRANDFATHER SQUEERS

"My grandfather Squeers," said The Raggedy
Man,
As he solemnly lighted his pipe and began—

"The most indestructible man, for his years,
And the grandest on earth, was my grandfather
Squeers!

"He said, when he rounded his threescore-and-ten,
'I've the hang of it now and can do it again!'

"He had frozen his heels so repeatedly, he
Could tell by them just what the weather would be;

"And would laugh and declare, 'while *the Almanac* would
Most falsely prognosticate, *he* never could!'

"Such a hale constitution had grandfather Squeers
That, though he'd used '*navy*' for sixty-odd years,

"He still chewed a dime's-worth six days of the
week,
While the seventh he passed with a chew in each
cheek.

GRANDFATHER SQUEERS

" Then my grandfather Squeers had a singular knack
Of sitting around on the small of his back,

"With his legs like a letter Y stretched o'er the grate
Wherein 'twas his custom to ex-pec-tor-ate.

"He was fond of tobacco in *manifold* ways,
And would sit on the door-step, of sunshiny days,

"And smoke leaf-tobacco he'd raised strictly for
The pipe he'd used all through The Mexican War."

And The Raggedy Man said, refilling the bowl
Of his *own* pipe and leisurely picking a coal

From the stove with his finger and thumb, "You can see
What a tee-nacious habit he's fastened on me!

And my grandfather Squeers took a special delight
In pruning his corns every Saturday night

With a horn-handled razor, whose edge he excused
By saying 'twas one that his grandfather used;

"And, though deeply etched in the haft of the same
Was the ever-euphonious Wostenholm's name,

"'Twas my grandfather's custom to boast of the blade
As 'A Seth Thomas razor—the best ever made!'

"No Old Settlers' Meeting, or Pioneers' Fair,
Was complete without grandfather Squeers in the chair,

"To lead off the program by telling folks how
'He used to shoot deer where the Court-House stands now'—

"How 'he felt, of a truth, to live over the past,
When the country was wild and unbroken and vast,

"'That the little log cabin was just plenty fine
For himself, his companion, and fambly of nine!—

GRANDFATHER SQUEERS

" 'When they didn't have even a pump, or a tin,
But drunk surface-water, year out and year in,

" 'From the old-fashioned gourd that was sweeter,
 by odds,
Than the goblets of gold at the lips of the gods!' "

Then The Raggedy Man paused to plaintively say
It was clockin' along to'rds the close of the day—

And he'd *ought* to get back to his work on the
 lawn,—
Then dreamily blubbered his pipe and went on:

"His teeth were imperfect—my grandfather owned
That he couldn't eat oysters unless they were
 'boned';

"And his eyes were so weak, and so feeble of
 sight,
He couldn't sleep with them unless, every night,

"He put on his spectacles—all he possessed,—
Three pairs—with his goggles on top of the rest.

"And my grandfather always, retiring at night,
Blew down the lamp-chimney to put out the light;

GRANDFATHER SQUEERS

"Then he'd curl up on edge like a shaving, in bed,
And puff and smoke pipes in his sleep, it is said:

"And would snore oftentimes, as the legends relate,
Till his folks were wrought up to a terrible state,—

"Then he'd snort, and rear up, and roll over; and there
In the subsequent hush they could hear him chew air.

"And so glaringly bald was the top of his head
That many's the time he has musingly said,

"As his eyes journeyed o'er its reflex in the glass,—
'I must set out a few signs of *Keep Off the Grass!*'

"So remarkably deaf was my grandfather Squeers
That he had to wear lightning-rods over his ears

"To even hear thunder—and oftentimes then
He was forced to request it to thunder again."

THE LITTLE TINY KICKSHAW

O THE little tiny kickshaw that Mither sent tae me,
'Tis sweeter than the sugar-plum that reepens on
   the tree,
Wi' denty flavorin's o' spice an' musky rosemarie,
The little tiny kickshaw that Mither sent tae me.

'Tis luscious wi' the stalen tang o' fruits frae ower
   the sea,
An' e'en its fragrance gars me laugh wi' langin'
   lip an' ee,
Till a' its frazen sheen o' white maun melten
   hinnie be—
Sae weel I luve the kickshaw that Mither sent tae
   me.

O I luve the tiny kickshaw, an' I smack my lips
   wi' glee,
 Aye mickle do I luve the taste o' sic a luxourie,
But maist I luve the luvein' han's that could the
   giftie gie
O' the little tiny kickshaw that Mither sent tae me.

THE LUGUBRIOUS WHING-WHANG

THE rhyme o' The Raggedy Man's 'at's best
    Is Tickle me, Love, in these Lonesome Ribs
'Cause that-un's the strangest of all o' the rest,
An' the worst to learn, an' the last one guessed,
An' the funniest one, an' the foolishest.—
    Tickle me, Love, in these Lonesome Ribs!

I don't know what in the world it means—
    Tickle me, Love, in these Lonesome Ribs!—
An' nen when I *tell* him I don't, he leans
Like he was a-grindin' on some machines
An' says: Ef I *don't*, w'y, I don't know *beans!*
    Tickle me, Love, in these Lonesome Ribs!

Out on the margin of Moonshine Land,
    Tickle me, Love, in these Lonesome Ribs!
Out where the Whing-Whang loves to stand,
Writing his name with his tail in the sand,
And swiping it out with his oogerish hand;
    Tickle me, Love, in these Lonesome Ribs!

THE LUGUBRIOUS WHING-WHANG

Is it the gibber of Gungs or Keeks?
>Tickle me, Love, in these Lonesome Ribs!

Or what *is* the sound that the Whing-Whang
>>seeks?—

Crouching low by the winding creeks,
And holding his breath for weeks and weeks!
>Tickle me, Love, in these Lonesome Ribs!

Aroint him the wraithest of wraithly things!
>Tickle me, Love, in these Lonesome Ribs!

'Tis a fair Whing-Whangess, with phosphor rings
And bridal-jewels of fangs and stings;
And she sits and as sadly and softly sings
As the mildewed whir of her own dead wings,—
>Tickle me, Dear,
>>Tickle me here,
>Tickle me, Love, in me Lonesome Ribs!

THE WAY THE BABY WOKE

And this is the way the baby woke:
  As when in deepest drops of dew
The shine and shadows sink and soak,
  The sweet eyes glimmered through and through
And eddyings and dimples broke
  About the lips, and no one knew
Or could divine the words they spoke—
And this is the way the baby woke.

McFEETERS' FOURTH

It was needless to say 'twas a glorious day,
And to boast of it all in that spread-eagle way
That our Forefathers had since the hour of the birth
Of this most patriotic republic on earth!
But 'twas justice, of course, to admit that the sight
Of the old Stars-and-Stripes was a thing of delight
In the eyes of a fellow, however he tried
To look on the day with a dignified pride
That meant not to brook any turbulent glee
Or riotous flourish of loud jubilee!

So argued McFeeters, all grim and severe,
Who the long night before, with a feeling of fear,
Had slumbered but fitfully, hearing the swish
Of the sky rocket over his roof, with the wish
That the boy-fiend who fired it were fast to the end
Of the stick to for ever and ever ascend!
Or to hopelessly ask why the boy with the horn
And its horrible havoc had ever been born!
Or to wish, in his wakefulness, staring aghast,
That this Fourth of July were as dead as the last!

McFEETERS' FOURTH

So, yesterday morning, McFeeters arose,
With a fire in his eyes, and a cold in his nose,
And a guttural voice in appropriate key
With a temper as gruff as a temper could be.
He growled at the servant he met on the stair,
Because he was whistling a national air,
And he growled at the maid on the balcony, who
Stood enrapt with the tune of "The Red-White-
    and-Blue"
That a band was discoursing like mad in the street,
With drumsticks that banged, and with cymbals
    that beat.

And he growled at his wife, as she buttoned his
    vest,
And applausively pinned a rosette on his breast
Of the national colors, and lured from his purse
Some change for the boys—for fire-crackers—or
    worse;
And she pointed with pride to a soldier in blue
In a frame on the wall, and the colors there, too;
And he felt, as he looked on the features, the glow
The painter found there twenty long years ago,

McFEETERS' FOURTH

And a passionate thrill in his breast, as he felt
Instinctively round for the sword in his belt.

What was it that hung like a mist o'er the room?—
The tumult without—and the music—the boom
Of the cannon—the blare of the bugle and fife?—
No matter!—McFeeters was kissing his wife,
And laughing and crying and waving his hat
Like a genuine soldier, and crazy, at that!
—*Was* it needless to say 'twas a glorious day
And to boast of it all in that spread-eagle way
That our Forefathers had since the hour of the birth
Of this most patriotic republic on earth?

LITTLE MANDY'S CHRISTMAS-TREE

Little Mandy and her Ma
'S porest folks you ever saw!—
Lived in porest house in town,
Where the fence 'uz all tore down.

And no front-door steps at all—
Ist a' old box 'g'inst the wall;
And no door-knob on the door
Outside.—*My!* but they 'uz pore!

Wuz no winder-shutters on,
And some of the *winders* gone,
And where *they* 'uz broke they'd pas'e
Ist brown paper 'crost the place.

Tell you! when it's *winter there*,
And the snow ist ever'where,
Little Mandy's Ma she say
'Spec' they'll freeze to death some day.

Wunst my Ma and me—when we
Be'n to church, and's goin' to be
Chris'mus purty soon,—we went
There—like the Committee sent.

LITTLE MANDY'S CHRISTMAS-TREE

And-sir! when we're in the door,
Wuz no carpet on the floor,
And no fire—and heels-and-head
Little Mandy's tucked in bed!

And her Ma telled *my* Ma she
Got no coffee but ist tea,
And fried mush—and's all they had
Sence her health broke down so bad

Nen Ma hug and hold me where
Little Mandy's layin' there;
And she kiss her, too, and nen
Mandy kiss my Ma again.

And my Ma she telled her *we*
Goin' to have a Chris'mus-Tree,
At the Sund'y School, 'at's fer
ALL the childern, and fer *her*.

Little Mandy *think*—nen she
Say, "What *is* a Chris'mus-Tree?"
Nen my Ma she gived *her* Ma
Somepin' 'at I never saw,

LITTLE MANDY'S CHRISTMAS-TREE

And say she *must* take it,—and
She ist maked her keep her hand
Wite close shut,—and nen she *kiss*
Her hand—shut ist like it is.

Nen we comed away. . . . And nen
When its Chris'mus Eve again,
And all of us childerns be
At the Church and Chris'mus-Tree —

And all git our toys and things
'At old Santy Claus he brings
And puts on the Tree;—wite where
The *big* Tree 'uz standin' there,

And the things 'uz all tooked down,
And the childerns, all in town,
Got their presents—nen we see
They's a *little* Chris'mus-Tree

Wite *behind* the *big* Tree—so
We can't see till *nen*, you know,—
And it's all ist loaded down
With the purtiest things in town!

LITTLE MANDY'S CHRISTMAS-TREE

And the teacher smile and say:
"This-here Tree 'at's hid away
It's marked '*Little Mandy's Tree.*'—
Little Mandy! Where is she?"

Nen nobody say a word.—
Stillest place you ever heard!—
Till a man tiptoe up where
Teacher's still a-waitin' there.

Nen the man he whispers, so
Ist the *Teacher* hears, you know.
Nen he tiptoe back and go
Out the big door—ist as slow!

. . . . .

Little Mandy, though, *she* don't
Answer—and Ma say "she won't
Never, though each year they'll be
'Little Mandy's Chris'mus-Tree'

Fer pore childern"—my Ma says—
And *Committee* say they guess
"Little Mandy's Tree" 'ull be
Bigger than the *other* Tree!

THE FUNNIEST THING IN THE WORLD

The funniest thing in the world, I know,
Is watchin' the monkeys 'at's in the show!—
Jumpin' an' runnin' an' racin' roun',
'Way up the top o' the pole; nen down!
First they're here, an' nen they're there,
An' ist a'most any an' ever'where!—
Screechin' an' scratchin' wherever they go,
They're the funniest thing in the world, I know!

They're the funniest thing in the world, I think:—
Funny to watch 'em eat an' drink;
Funny to watch 'em a-watchin' us,
An' actin' 'most like grown folks does!—
Funny to watch 'em p'tend to be
Skeerd at their tail 'at they happen to see;—
But the funniest thing in the world they do
Is never to laugh, like me an' you!

LITTLE JOHNTS'S CHRIS'MUS

We got it up a-purpose, jes fer little Johnts, you
    know;
His mother was so pore an' all, an' had to man-
    age so—
Jes bein' a War-widder, an' her pension mighty
    slim,
She'd take in weavin', er work out, er anything
    fer him!

An' little Johnts was puny-like—but law, *the nerve*
    he had!—
You'd want to kindo' pity him, but couldn't, very
    bad,—
His pants o' army-blanket an' his coat o' faded
    blue
Kep' hintin' of his father like, an' pity wouldn't do!

So we collogued together, onc't, one winter-time,
    'at we—
Jes me an' mother an' the girls, an' Wilse, John-
    Jack an' Free—

LITTLE JOHNTS'S CHRIS'MUS

Would jine an' git up little Johnts, by time 'at
    Chris'mus come,
Some sort o' doin's, don't you know, 'at would
    su'prise him some.

An' so, all on the quiet, Mother she turns in an'
    gits
Some blue-janes—cuts an' makes a suit; an' then
    sets down an' knits
A pair o' little galluses to go 'long with the rest—
An' putts in a red-flannen back, an' buckle on the
    vest.—

The little feller'd be'n so much around our house,
    you see,
An' be'n sich he'p to her an' all, an' handy as
    could be,
'At Mother couldn't do too much fer little Johnts—
    No, *Sir!*
She ust to jes declare 'at "he was meat-an'-drink
    to her!"

LITTLE JOHNTS'S CHRIS'MUS

An' Piney, Lide, an' Madaline they watch their
    chance an' rid
To Fountaintown with Lijey's folks; an' bought
    a book, they did,
O' fairy tales, with pictur's in; an' got a little pair
O' red-top boots 'at John-Jack said he'd be'n a-
    pricin' there.

An' Lide got him a little sword, an' Madaline, a
    drum;
An' shootin'-crackers—Lawzy-day! an' they're so
    danger-some!
An' Piney, ever' time the rest 'ud buy some other
    toy,
She'd take an' turn in then an' buy more candy
    fer the boy!

"Well," thinks-says-I, when they got back, "*your*
    pocket-books is dry!"—
But little Johnts was there hisse'f that afternoon,
    so I—
Well, *all* of us kep' mighty mum, tel we got him
    away
By tellin' him be shore an' come to-morry—Chris'-
    mus Day—

LITTLE JOHNTS'S CHRIS'MUS

An' fetch *his mother* 'long with him! An' how he scud acrost
The fields—his towhead, in the dusk, jes like a streak o' frost!—
His comfert fluttern as he run—an' old Tige, don't you know,
A-jumpin' high for rabbits an' a ploughin' up the snow!

It must 'a' be'n 'most *ten* that night afore we got to bed—
With Wilse an' John-Jack he'ppin' us; an' Freeman in the shed,
An' Lide out with the lantern while he trimmed the Chris'mus Tree
Out of a little scrub-oak-top 'at suited to a "T"!

All night I dreamp' o' hearin' things a-skulkin' round the place—
An' "Old Kriss," with his whiskers off, an' freckles on his face—
An' reindeers, shaped like shavin'-hosses at the cooper-shop,
A-stickin' down the chimbly, with their heels out at the top!

LITTLE JOHNTS'S CHRIS'MUS

By time 'at Mother got me up 'twas plum daylight an' more—
The front yard full o' neighbors all a-crowdin' round the door,
With Johnts's mother leadin'; yes—an' little Johnts hisse'f,
Set up on Freeman's shoulder, like a jug up on the she'f!

Of course I can't describe it when they all got in to where
We'd conjered up the Chris'mus-Tree an' all the fixin's there!—
Fer all the shouts o' laughture—clappin' hands, an' crackin' jokes,
Was heap o' kissin' goin' on amongst the womenfolks:—

Fer, lo-behold-ye! there they had that young-un!— An' his chin
A-wobblin'-like;—an', shore enough, at last he started in—
An'—sich another bellerin', in all my mortal days,
I never heerd, er 'spect to hear, in woe's app'inted ways!

LITTLE JOHNTS'S CHRIS'MUS

An' Mother grabs him up an' says: "It's more'n
    he can bear—
It's all too *suddent* fer the child, an' too su'prisin'!
    —*There!*"
"Oh, no it ain't"—sobbed little Johnts—"I ain't
    su'prised—but I'm
A-cryin' 'cause I watched you all, an' knowed it
    all the time!"

THE ORCHARD LANDS OF LONG AGO

The orchard lands of Long Ago!
O drowsy winds, awake, and blow
The snowy blossoms back to me,
And all the buds that used to be!
Blow back along the grassy ways
Of truant feet, and lift the haze
Of happy summer from the trees
That trail their tresses in the seas
Of grain that float and overflow
The orchard lands of Long Ago!

Blow back the melody that slips
In lazy laughter from the lips
That marvel much if any kiss
Is sweeter than the apple's is.
Blow back the twitter of the birds—
The lisp, the titter, and the words

THE ORCHARD LANDS OF LONG AGO

Of merriment that found the shine
Of summer-time a glorious wine
That drenched the leaves that loved it so
In orchard lands of Long Ago!

O memory! alight and sing
Where rosy-bellied pippins cling,
And golden russets glint and gleam,
As, in the old Arabian dream,
The fruits of that enchanted tree
The glad Aladdin robbed for me!
And, drowsy winds, awake and fan
My blood as when it overran
A heart ripe as the apples grow
In orchard lands of Long Ago!

THE BOYS' CANDIDATE

Las' time 'at Uncle Sidney come,
He bringed a watermelon home—
　An' half the boys in town
Come taggin' after him.—An' he
Says, when we et it,—"*Gracious me!
　'S the boy-house fell down?*"

THE BUMBLEBEE

You better not fool with a Bumblebee!—
Ef you don't think they can sting—you'll see!
They're lazy to look at, an' kindo' go
Buzzin' an' bummin' aroun' so slow,
An' ac' so slouchy an' all fagged out,
Danglin' their legs as they drone about
The hollyhawks 'at they can't climb in
'Ithout ist a-tumble-un out ag'in!
Wunst I watched one climb clean 'way
In a jimson-blossom, I did, one day,—
An' I ist grabbed it—an' nen let go—
An' *"Ooh-ooh! Honey! I told ye so!"*
Says the Raggedy Man; an' he ist run
An' pullt out the stinger, an' don't laugh none
An' says: "They *has* be'n folks, I guess,
'At thought I wuz prejudust, more er less,—
Yit I still muntain 'at a Bumblebee
Wears out his welcome too quick fer me!"

HE CALLED HER IN

I

He called her in from me and shut the door.
And she so loved the sunshine and the sky!—
She loved them even better yet than I
That ne'er knew dearth of them—my mother dead
Nature had nursed me in her lap instead:
And I had grown a dark and eerie child
That rarely smiled,
Save when, shut all alone in grasses high,
Looking straight up in God's great lonesome sky
And coaxing Mother to smile back on me.
 Twas lying thus, this fair girl suddenly
Came on me, nestled in the fields beside
A pleasant-seeming home, with doorway wide—
The sunshine beating in upon the floor
Like golden rain.—
O sweet, sweet face above me, turn again
And leave me! I had cried, but that an ache
Within my throat so gripped it I could make

HE CALLED HER IN

No sound but a thick sobbing.   Cowering so,
I felt her light hand laid
Upon my hair—a touch that ne'er before
Had tamed me thus, all soothed and unafraid—
It seemed the touch the children used to know
When Christ was here, so dear it was—so dear,—
At once I loved her as the leaves love dew
In midmost summer when the days are new.
Barely an hour I knew her, yet a curl
Of silken sunshine did she clip for me
Out of the bright May-morning of her hair,
And bound and gave it to me laughingly,
And caught my hands and called me "*Little girl*,"
Tiptoeing, as she spoke, to kiss me there!
And I stood dazed and dumb for very stress
Of my great happiness.
She plucked me by the gown, nor saw how mean
The raiment—drew me with her everywhere:
Smothered her face in tufts of grasses green:
Put up her dainty hands and peeped between
Her fingers at the blossoms—crooned and talked
To them in strange, glad whispers, as we walked,—
Said *this* one was her angel mother—*this*,
Her baby-sister—come back, for a kiss,

HE CALLED HER IN

Clean from the Good-World!—smiled and kissed
    them, then
Closed her soft eyes and kissed them o'er again.
And so did she beguile me—so we played,—
She was the dazzling Shine—I, the dark Shade—
And we did mingle like to these, and thus,
Together, made
The perfect summer, pure and glorious.
So blent we, till a harsh voice broke upon
Our happiness.—She, startled as a fawn,
Cried, "Oh, 'tis Father!"—all the blossoms gone
From out her cheeks as those from out her grasp.—
Harsher the voice came:—She could only gasp
Affrightedly, "Good-bye!—good-bye! good-
    bye!"
And lo, I stood alone, with that harsh cry
Ringing a new and unknown sense of shame
Through soul and frame,
And, with wet eyes, repeating o'er and o'er,—
"He called her in from me and shut the door!"

HE CALLED HER IN

II

He called her in from me and shut the door!
And I went wandering alone again—
So lonely—O so very lonely then,
I thought no little sallow star, alone
In all a world of twilight, e'er had known
Such utter loneliness. But that I wore
Above my heart that gleaming tress of hair
To lighten up the night of my despair,
I think I might have groped into my grave
Nor cared to wave
The ferns above it with a breath of prayer.
And how I hungered for the sweet, sweet face
That bent above me in my hiding-place
That day amid the grasses there beside
Her pleasant home!—"Her *pleasant* home!" I
    sighed,
Remembering;—then shut my teeth and feigned
The harsh voice calling *me*,—then clinched my
    nails
So deeply in my palms, the sharp wounds pained,
And tossed my face toward heaven, as one who
    pales

HE CALLED HER IN

In splendid martyrdom, with soul serene,
As near to God as high the guillotine.
And I had *envied* her? Not that—O no!
But I had longed for some sweet haven so!—
Wherein the tempest-beaten heart might ride
Sometimes at peaceful anchor, and abide
Where those that loved me touched me with their
    hands,
And looked upon me with glad eyes, and slipped
Smooth fingers o'er my brow, and lulled the strands
Of my wild tresses, as they backward tipped
My yearning face and kissed it satisfied.
Then bitterly I murmured as before,—
"He called her in from me and shut the door!"

III

He called her in from me and shut the door!
After long struggling with my pride and pain—
A weary while it seemed, in which the more
I held myself from her, the greater fain
Was I to look upon her face again;—
At last—at last—half conscious where my feet
Were faring, I stood waist-deep in the sweet
Green grasses there where she
First came to me.—

HE CALLED HER IN

The very blossoms she had plucked that day,
And, at her father's voice, had cast away,
Around me lay,
Still bright and blooming in these eyes of mine;
And as I gathered each one eagerly,
I pressed it to my lips and drank the wine
Her kisses left there for the honey-bee.
Then, after I had laid them with the tress
Of her bright hair with lingering tenderness,
I, turning, crept on to the hedge that bound
Her pleasant-seeming home—but all around
Was never sign of her!—The windows all
Were blinded; and I heard no rippling fall
Of her glad laugh, nor any harsh voice call;—
But, clutching to the tangled grasses, caught
A sound as though a strong man bowed his head
And sobbed alone—unloved—uncomforted!—
And then straightway before
My tearless eyes, all vividly, was wrought
A vision that is with me evermore:—
A little girl that lies asleep, nor hears
Nor heeds not any voice nor fall of tears.—
And I sit singing o'er and o'er and o'er,—
"God called her in from him and shut the door!

THE BOY-FRIEND

CLARENCE, my boy-friend, hale and strong!
　O he is as jolly as he is young;
And all of the laughs of the lyre belong
　To the boy all unsung:

So I want to sing something in his behalf—
　To clang some chords, for the good it is
To know he is near, and to have the laugh
　Of that wholesome voice of his.

I want to tell him in gentler ways
　Than prose may do, that the arms of rhyme
Warm and tender with tuneful praise,
　Are about him all the time.

I want him to know that the quietest nights
　We have passed together are yet with me,
Roistering over the old delights
　That were born of his company.

THE BOY-FRIEND

I want him to know how my soul esteems
    The fairy stories of Andersen,
And the glad translations of all the themes
    Of the hearts of boyish men.

Want him to know that my fancy flows,
    With the lilt of a dear old-fashioned tune
Through "Lewis Carroll's" poemly prose,
    And the tale of "The Bold Dragoon."

O this is the Prince that I would sing—
    Would drape and garnish in velvet line,
Since courtlier far than any king
    Is this brave boy-friend of mine.

WHEN THE WORLD BU'STS THROUGH

[*Casually Suggested by an Earthquake*]

WHERE's a boy a-goin',
  An' what's he goin' to do,
An' how's he goin' to do it,
  When the world bu'sts through?
Ma she says "she can't tell
  What we're comin' to!"
An' Pop says "he's ist skeered
  Clean—plum—through!"

S'pose we'd be a-playin'
  Out in the street,
An' the ground 'ud split up
  'Bout forty feet!—
Ma says "she ist knows
  We 'ud tumble in";
An' Pop says "he bets you
  Nen we wouldn't grin!"

S'pose we'd ist be 'tendin'
  Like we had a show,
Down in the stable
  Where we mustn' go,—

WHEN THE WORLD BU'STS THROUGH

Ma says, "The earthquake
  Might make it fall";
An' Pop says, "More'n like
  Swaller barn an' all!"

Landy! ef we both wuz
  Runnin' 'way from school,
Out in the shady woods
  Where it's all so cool!—
Ma says "a big tree
  Might sqush our head";
An' Pop says, "Chop 'em out
  Both—killed—dead!"

But where's a boy goin',
  An' what's he goin' to do,
An' how's he goin' to do it,
  Ef the world bu'sts through?
Ma she says "she can't tell
  What we're comin' to!"
An' Pop says "he's ist skeered
  Clean—plum—through!"

A PROSPECTIVE GLIMPSE

Janey Pettibone's the best
Little girl an' purtiest
In this town! an' lives next door,
Up-stairs over their old store.

Little Janey Pettibone
An' her Ma lives all alone,—
'Cause her Pa broke up, an' nen
Died 'cause they ain't rich again.

Little Janey's Ma she sews
Fer my Ma sometimes, an' goes
An' gives music-lessuns—where
People's got pianers there.

But when Janey Pettibone
Grows an' grows, like I'm a growin
Nen *I'm* go' to keep a store,
An' sell things—an' sell some more

Till I'm ist as rich!—An' nen
Her Ma can be rich again,—
Ef *I'm* rich enough to own
Little Janey Pettibone!

THE OLD TRAMP

A' OLD Tramp slep' in our stable wunst,
  An' The Raggedy Man he caught
An' roust him up, an' chased him off
  Clean out through our back lot!

An' th' old Tramp hollered back an' said,—
  "You're a *purty* man!—*You* air!—
With a pair o' eyes like two fried eggs,
  An' a nose like a Bartlutt pear!"

CURLY LOCKS

Curly Locks! Curly Locks! wilt thou be mine?
*Thou shalt not wash the dishes, nor yet feed the
    swine,—*
But sit on a cushion and sew a fine seam,
And feast upon strawberries, sugar and cream.

Curly Locks! Curly Locks! wilt thou be mine?
The throb of my heart is in every line,
And the pulse of a passion as airy and glad
In its musical beat as the little Prince had!

Thou shalt not wash the dishes, nor yet feed the
    swine!—
O I'll dapple thy hands with these kisses of mine
Till the pink of the nail of each finger shall be
As a little pet blush in full blossom for me.

But sit on a cushion and sew a fine seam,
And thou shalt have fabric as fair as a dream,—
The red of my veins, and the white of my love,
And the gold of my joy for the braiding thereof.

CURLY LOCKS

And feast upon strawberries, sugar and cream
From a service of silver, with jewels agleam,—
At thy feet will I bide, at thy beck will I rise,
And twinkle my soul in the night of thine eyes!

Curly Locks! Curly Locks! wilt thou be mine?
Thou shalt not wash the dishes, nor yet feed the swine,—
But sit on a cushion and sew a fine seam,
And feast upon strawberries, sugar and cream.

THE PET COON

Noey Bixler ketched him, an' fetched him in to me
    When he's ist a little teenty-weenty baby-coon
'Bout as big as little pups, an' tied him to a tree;
    An' Pa gived Noey fifty cents, when he come home at noon.
Nen he buyed a chain fer him, an' little collar, too,
    An' sawed a hole in a' old tub an' turnt it upside down;
An' little feller'd stay in there and won't come out fer you—
    'Tendin' like he's kindo' skeered o' boys 'at lives in town.

Now he ain't afeard a bit! he's ist so fat an' tame,
    We on'y chain him up at night, to save the little chicks.
Holler "Greedy! Greedy!" to him, an' he knows his name,
    An' here he'll come a-waddle-un, up fer any tricks!

THE PET COON

He'll climb up my leg, he will, an' waller in my lap,
  An' poke his little black paws 'way in my pockets where
They's beechnuts, er chinkypins, er any little scrap
  Of anything 'at's good to eat—an' *he* don't care!

An' he's as spunky as you please, an' don't like dogs at all.—
  Billy Miller's black-an'-tan tackled him one day,
An' "Greedy" he ist kindo' doubled all up like a ball,
  An' Billy's dog he gived a yelp er two an' runned away!
An' nen when Billy fighted me, an' hit me with a bone,
  An' Ma she purt' nigh ketched him as he dodged an' scooted through
The fence, she says, "You better let my little boy alone,
  Or 'Greedy,' next he whips yer dog, shall whip you, too!"

A NONSENSE RHYME

>Ringlety-jing!
>And what will we sing?
>Some little crinkety-crankety thing
>>That rhymes and chimes,
>>And skips, sometimes,
>As though wound up with a kink in the spring.

>>Grunkety-krung!
>>And chunkety-plung!
>Sing the song that the bullfrog sung,—
>>>A song of the soul
>>>Of a mad tadpole
>>That met his fate in a leaky bowl:
>And it's O for the first false wiggle he made
>In a sea of pale pink lemonade!
>>And it's O for the thirst
>>>Within him pent,
>>And the hopes that burst
>>>As his reason went—
>When his strong arm failed and his strength was spent!

A NONSENSE RHYME

Sing, O sing
 Of the things that cling,
And the claws that clutch and the fangs that sting—
 Till the tadpole's tongue
 And his tail upflung
Quavered and failed with a song unsung!
 O the dank despair in the rank morass,
  Where the crawfish crouch in the cringing
   grass,
 And the long limp rune of the loon wails on
  For the mad, sad soul
  Of a bad tadpole
    Forever lost and gone!

 Jinglety-jee!
 And now we'll see
What the last of the lay shall be,
 As the dismal tip of the tune, O friends,
 Swoons away and the long tale ends.
  And it's O and alack!
   For the tangled legs
   And the spangled back
    Of the green grig's eggs,

A NONSENSE RHYME

    And the unstrung strain
      Of the strange refrain
That the winds wind up like a strand of rain!

    And it's O,
        Also,
  For the ears wreathed low,
Like a laurel-wreath on the lifted brow
Of the frog that chants of the why and how,
    And the wherefore too, and the thus and so
      Of the wail he weaves in a woof of woe!
Twangle, then, with your wrangling strings,
The tinkling links of a thousand things!
And clang the pang of a maddening moan
Till the Echo, hid in a land unknown,
    Shall leap as he hears, and hoot and hoo
    Like the wretched wraith of a Whoopty-Doo!

NAUGHTY CLAUDE

When Little Claude was naughty wunst
   At dinner-time, an' said
He won't say "*Thank you*" to his Ma,
   She maked him go to bed
An' stay two hours an' not git up,—
   So when the clock struck Two,
Nen Claude says,—"Thank you, Mr. Clock
   I'm much obleeged to you!"

THE OLD, OLD WISH

Last night, in some lost mood of meditation,
  The while my dreamy vision ranged the far
Unfathomable arches of creation,
        I saw a falling star:

And as my eyes swept round the path it embered
  With the swift-dying glory of its glow,
With sudden intuition I remembered,
        A wish of long ago—

A wish that, were it made—so ran the fancy
  Of credulous young lover and of lass—
As fell a star, by some strange necromancy,
        Would surely come to pass.

And, of itself, the wish, reiterated
  A thousand times in youth, flashed o'er my brain,
And, like the star, as soon obliterated,
        Dropped into night again.

THE OLD, OLD WISH

For my old heart had wished for the unending
    Devotion of a little maid of nine—
And that the girl-heart, with the woman's blend
      ing,
            Might be forever mine.

And so it was, with eyelids raised, and weighty
    With ripest clusterings of sorrow's dew,
I cried aloud through heaven: "O little Katie!
            When will my wish come true?'

"THE PREACHER'S BOY"

I RICKOLLECT the little tad, back, years and years ago—
"The Preacher's Boy" that every one despised and hated so!
A meek-faced little feller, with white eyes and foxy hair,
And a look like he expected ser'ous trouble everywhere:
A sort o' fixed expression of suspicion in his glance;
His bare-feet always scratched with briers; and green stains on his pants;
Molasses-marks along his sleeves; his cap-rim turned behind—
And so it is "The Preacher's Boy" is brought again to mind!

My fancy even brings the sly marauder back so plain,
I see him jump our garden-fence and slip off down the lane;

"THE PREACHER'S BOY"

And I seem to holler at him and git back the old reply:
"Oh, no: your peaches is too green fer such a worm as I!"
Fer he scorned his father's phrases—every holy one he had—
"As good a man," folks put it, "as that boy of his was bad!"
And again from their old buggy-shed, I hear the "rod unspared"—
Of course that never "spoiled the child" for which nobody cared!

If any neighbor ever found his gate without a latch,
Or rines around the edges of his watermelon-patch;
His pasture-bars left open; or his pump-spout chocked with clay,
He'd swear 'twas "that infernal Preacher's Boy," right away!
When strings was stretched acrost the street at night, and some one got
An everlastin' tumble, and his nose broke, like as not,

"THE PREACHER'S BOY"

And laid it on "The Preacher's Boy"—no powers,
    low ner high,
Could ever quite substantiate that boy's alibi!

And did *nobody* like the boy?—Well, all the *pets*
    in town
Would eat out of his fingers; and canaries would
    come down
And leave their swingin' perches and their fish-
    bone jist to pick
The little warty knuckles that the dogs would leap
    to lick.—
No little snarlin', snappin' fiste but what would
    leave his bone
To foller, ef *he* whistled, in that tantalizin' tone
That made the goods-box whittler blasphemeously
    protest
"He couldn't tell, 'twixt dog and boy, which one
    was ornriest!"

'Twas such a little cur as this, onc't, when the
    crowd was thick
Along the streets, a drunken corner-loafer tried to
    kick,

"THE PREACHER'S BOY"

When a sudden foot behind him tripped him up,
    and falling so
He "marked his man," and jerked his gun—
    drawed up and let 'er go!
And the crowd swarmed round the victim—holding close against his breast
The little dog unharmed, in arms that still, as they caressed,
Grew rigid in their last embrace, as with a smile of joy
He recognized the dog was saved. So died "The Preacher's Boy"!
When it appeared, before the Squire, that fatal pistol-ball
Was fired at "a dangerous beast," and not the boy at all,
And the facts set forth established—it was like-befittin' then
To order out a possy of the "city councilmen"
To kill *the dog!* But, strange to tell, they searched the country round,
And never hide-ner-hair of that "said" dog was ever found!

"THE PREACHER'S BOY"

And, somehow, *then* I sorto' thought—and halfway think, *to-day*—
The spirit of "The Preacher's Boy" had whistled him away.

AN IMPETUOUS RESOLVE

When little Dickie Swope's a man,
   He's go' to be a Sailor;
An' little Hamey Tincher, he's
   A-go' to be a Tailor:
Bud Mitchell, he's a-go' to be
   A stylish Carriage-Maker;
An' when *I* grow a grea'-big man,
   I'm go' to be a Baker!

An' Dick'll buy his sailor-suit
   O' Hame; an' Hame'll take it
An' buy as fine a double-rig
   As ever Bud kin make it:
An' nen all three'll drive roun' fer me
   An' we'll drive off togevver,
A-slingin' pie-crust 'long the road
   Ferever an' ferever!

A SUDDEN SHOWER

BAREFOOTED boys scud up the street
   Or scurry under sheltering sheds;
   And school-girl faces, pale and sweet,
Gleam from the shawls about their heads.

Doors bang; and mother-voices call
   From alien homes; and rusty gates
Are slammed; and high above it all,
   The thunder grim reverberates.

And then, abrupt,—the rain! the rain!—
   The earth lies gasping; and the eyes
Behind the streaming window-pane
   Smile at the trouble of the skies.

The highway smokes; sharp echoes ring;
   The cattle bawl and cow-bells clank;
And into town comes galloping
   The farmer's horse, with steaming flank

A SUDDEN SHOWER

The swallow dips beneath the eaves
    And flirts his plumes and folds his wings;
And under the Catawba leaves
    The caterpillar curls and clings.

The bumblebee is pelted down
    The wet stem of the hollyhock;
And sullenly, in spattered brown,
    The cricket leaps the garden-walk.

Within, the baby claps his hands
    And crows with rapture strange and vague
Without, beneath the rose-bush stands
    A dripping rooster on one leg.

THE HUNTER BOY

Hunter Boy of Hazelwood—
Happier than Robin Hood!
Dance across the green, and stand
Suddenly, with lifted hand
Shading eager eyes, and be
Thus content to capture me!—
Cease thy quest for wilder prey
Than my willing heart to-day!

Hunter Boy! with belt and bow,
Bide with me, or let me go,
An thou wilt, in wake of thee,
Questing for my mine infancy!
With thy glad face in the sun,
Let thy laughter overrun
Thy ripe lips, until mine own
Answer, ringing, tone for tone!

THE HUNTER BOY

O my Hunter! tilt the cup
Of thy silver bugle up,
And like wine pour out for me
All its limpid melody!
Pout thy happy lips and blare
Music's kisses everywhere—
Whiff o'er forest, field and town
Tufts of tune like thistle-down!
    O to go, as once I could,
      Hunter Boy of Hazelwood!

THE MAN IN THE MOON

SAID The Raggedy Man, on a hot afternoon:
  My!
      Sakes!
           What a lot o' mistakes
Some little folks makes on The Man in the Moon!
But people that's be'n up to *see* him, like *me*,
And calls on him frequent and intimuttly,
Might drop a few facts that would interest you
  Clean!
      Through!—
          If you wanted 'em to—
Some *actual* facts that might interest you!

O The Man in the Moon has a crick in his back;
  Whee!
      Whimm!
          Ain't you sorry for him?
And a mole on his nose that is purple and black;
And his eyes are so weak that they water and run
If he dares to *dream* even he looks at the sun,—

THE MAN IN THE MOON

So he jes dreams of stars, as the doctors advise—
 My!
   Eyes!
     But isn't he wise—
To jes dream of stars, as the doctors advise?

And The Man in the Moon has a boil on his ear—
 Whee!
   Whing!
     What a singular thing!
I know! but these facts are authentic, my dear,—
There's a boil on his ear; and a corn on his chin—
He calls it a dimple—but dimples stick in—
Yet it might be a dimple turned over, you know!
 Whang!
   Ho!
     Why, certainly so!—
It might be a dimple turned over, you know!

And The Man in the Moon has a rheumatic knee—
 Gee!
   Whizz!
     What a pity that is!
And his toes have worked round where his heels
  ought to be.—

THE MAN IN THE MOON

So whenever he wants to go North he goes *South*,
And comes back with porridge-crumbs all round
 his mouth,
And he brushes them off with a Japanese fan,
 Whing!
  Whann!
   What a marvellous man!
  What a very remarkably marvellous man!

And The Man in the Moon, sighed The Raggedy
 Man,
 Gits!
  So!
   Sullonesome, you know,—
Up there by hisse'f sence creation began!—
That when I call on him and then come away,
He grabs me and holds me and begs me to stay,—
Till—*Well!* if it wasn't fer *Jimmy-cum-jim*,
 Dadd!
  Limb!
   I'd go pardners with him—
 Jes jump my job here and be pardners with
  him!

A CHILD'S HOME—LONG AGO

Even as the gas-flames flicker to and fro,
The Old Man's wavering fancies leap and glow,—
As o'er the vision, like a mirage, falls
The old log cabin with its dingy walls,
And crippled chimney with its crutch-like prop
Beneath a sagging shoulder at the top:
The coonskin battened fast on either side—
The wisps of leaf-tobacco—"cut-and-dried";
The yellow strands of quartered apples, hung
In rich festoons that tangle in among
The morning-glory vines that clamber o'er
The little clapboard roof above the door:
The old well-sweep that drops a courtesy
To every thirsting soul so graciously,
The stranger, as he drains the dripping gourd,
Intuitively mumurs, "Thank the Lord!"
Again through mists of memory arise
The simple scenes of home before the eyes:—

A CHILD'S HOME—LONG AGO

The happy mother, humming, with her wheel,
The dear old melodies that used to steal
So drowsily upon the summer air,
The house-dog hid his bone, forgot his care,
And nestled at her feet, to dream, perchance,
Some cooling dream of winter-time romance:
The square of sunshine through the open door
That notched its edge across the puncheon floor
And made a golden coverlet whereon
The god of slumber had a picture drawn
Of Babyhood, in all the loveliness
Of dimpled cheek and limb and linsey dress:
The bough-filled fireplace, and the mantel wide
Its fire-scorched ankles stretched on either side,
Where, perched upon its shoulders 'neath the joist
The old clock hiccoughed, harsh and husky-voiced
And snarled the premonition, dire and dread,
When it should hammer Time upon the head:
Tomatoes, red and yellow, in a row,
Preserved not then for diet, but for show,—
Like rare and precious jewels in the rough
Whose worth was not appraised at half enough:
The jars of jelly, with their dusty tops;
The bunch of pennyroyal; the cordial drops;

A CHILD'S HOME—LONG AGO

The flask of camphor, and the vial of squills,
The box of buttons, garden-seeds, and pills;
And, ending all the mantel's bric-à-brac,
The old, time-honored "Family Almanack."
And memory, with a mother's touch of love,
Climbs with us to the dusky loft above,
Where drowsily we trail our fingers in
The mealy treasures of the harvest bin;
And, feeling with our hands the open track,
We pat the bag of barley on the back;
And, groping onward through the mellow gloom
We catch the hidden apple's faint perfume,
And, mingling with it, fragrant hints of pear
And musky melon ripening somewhere.
Again we stretch our limbs upon the bed
Where first our simple childish prayers were said
And while, without, the gallant cricket trills
A challenge to the solemn whippoorwills,
And, filing on the chorus with his glee,
The katydid whets all the harmony
To feather-edge of incoherent song,
We drop asleep, and peacefully along
The current of our dreams we glide away
To the dim harbor of another day.

BILLY GOODIN'

"A big piece o' pie, and a big piece o' puddin'—
I laid it all by fer little Billy Goodin'!"
BOY-POET.

LOOK so neat an' sweet in all yer frills an' fancy pleatin'!
Better shet yer kitchen, though, afore you go to Meetin'!—
  Better hide yer mince-meat an' stewed fruit an' plums!
  Better hide yer pound-cake an' bresh away the crumbs!
  Better hide yer cubbord-key when Billy Goodin' comes,
      A-eatin'! an' a-eatin'! an' a-eatin'!

BILLY GOODIN'

Sight o' Sund'y-doin's done 'at ain't done in
    Meetin'!
Sun acrost yer garden-patch a-pourin' an' a-beatin';
  Meller apples drappin' in the weeds an' roun'
    the groun'—
  Clingstones an' sugar-pears a-ist a-plunkin'
    down!—
  Better kindo' comb the grass 'fore Billy comes
    aroun',
        A-eatin'! an' a-eatin'! an' a-eatin'!

Billy Goodin' ain't a-go' to go to any Meetin'!
We 'ull watch an' ketch an' give the little sneak a
    beatin'!—
  Better hint *we* want'o stay 'n' snoop yer grapes
    an' plums!
  Better eat 'em all yerse'f an' suck yer stingy
    thumbs!—
  Won't be nothin' anyhow when Billy Goodin'
    comes!
        A-eatin'! an' a-eatin'! an' a-eatin'!

A PASSING HAIL

LET us rest ourselves a bit!
Worry?—wave your hand to it—
Kiss your finger tips, and smile
It farewell a little while.

Weary of the weary way
We have come from Yesterday,
Let us fret us not, instead,
Of the weary way ahead.

Let us pause and catch our breath
On the hither side of death,
While we see the tender shoots
Of the grasses—not the roots,—

While we yet look down—not up—
To seek out the buttercup
And the daisy where they wave
O'er the green home of the grave.

A PASSING HAIL

Let us launch us smoothly on
The soft billows of the lawn,
And drift out across the main
Of our childish dreams again:

Voyage off, beneath the trees,
O'er the field's enchanted seas,
Where the lilies are our sails,
And our sea-gulls, nightingales:

Where no wilder storm shall beat
Than the wind that waves the wheat,
And no tempest-burst above
The old laughs we used to love:

Lose all troubles—gain release,
Languor, and exceeding peace,
Cruising idly o'er the vast,
Calm mid-ocean of the Past.

Let us rest ourselves a bit!
Worry?—Wave your hand to it—
Kiss your finger-tips, and smile
It farewell a little while.

PRIOR TO MISS BELLE'S APPEAR
ANCE

WHAT makes you come *here* fer, Mister,
   So much to *our* house?—*Say?*
Come to see our big sister!—
An' Charley he says 'at you kissed her
   An' he ketched you, th'uther day!—
Didn' you, Charley?—But we p'omised Belle
   An' crossed our heart to never tell—
'Cause *she* gived us some o' them-er
Chawk'lut-drops 'at you bringed to her!

Charley he's my little b'uther—
   An' we has a-mostest fun,
Don't we, Charley?—Our Muther,
Whenever we whips one-anuther,
   Tries to whip *us*—an' we *run*—
Don't we, Charley?—An' nen, bime-by,
Nen she gives us cake—an' pie—
Don't she, Charley?—when we come in
An' p'omise never to do it ag'in!

PRIOR TO MISS BELLE'S APPEARANCE

He's named Charley.—I'm *Willie*—
   An' I'm got the purtiest name!
But Uncle Bob *he* calls me "Billy"—
Don't he, Charley?—'N' our filly
   We named "Billy," the same
Ist like me! An' our Ma said
'At "Bob puts foolishnuss into our head!"—
Didn' she, Charley?—An' *she* don't know
Much about *boys!* 'Cause Bob said so!

Baby's a funniest feller!
   Nain't no hair on his head—
Is they, Charley?—It's meller
Wite up there! An' ef Belle er
   Us ask wus *we* that way, Ma said,—
"Yes; an' yer *Pa's* head wuz soft as that,
An' it's that way yet!"—An' Pa grabs his hat
An' says, "Yes, childern, she's right about Pa—
'Cause that's the reason he married yer Ma!"

An' our Ma says 'at "Belle couldn'
   Ketch nothin' at all but ist '*bows*'*!*"—
An' *Pa* says 'at "you're soft as puddun!"—
An' *Uncle Bob* says "you're a good-un—
   'Cause he can tell by yer nose!"—

PRIOR TO MISS BELLE'S APPEARANCE

Didn' he, Charley?—An' when Belle'll play
In the poller on th' pianer, some day,
Bob makes up funny songs about you,
Till she gits mad—like he wants her to!

Our sister *Fanny* she's 'leven
   Years old! 'At's mucher 'an *I*—
Ain't it, Charley? . . . I'm seven!—
But our sister Fanny's in *heaven!*
   Nere's where you go ef you die!—
Don't you, Charley?—Nen you has *wings*—
Ist like Fanny!—an' *purtiest things!*—
Don't you, Charley?—An' nen you can *fly*—
Ist fly—an' *ever'*thing! . . . Wisht *I'd* die!

SONG—FOR NOVEMBER

While skies glint bright with bluest light
    Through clouds that race o'er field and town
And leaves go dancing left and right,
    And orchard apples tumble down;
While school-girls sweet, in lane or street,
    Lean 'gainst the wind and feel and hear
Its glad heart like a lover's beat,—
    So reigns the rapture of the year.

Then ho! and hey! and whoop-hooray!
    Though winter clouds be looming,
Remember a November day
Is merrier than mildest May
    With all her blossoms blooming.

While birds in scattered flight are blown
    Aloft and lost in bosky mist,
And truant boys scud home alone
    'Neath skies of gold and amethyst;

SONG—FOR NOVEMBER

While twilight falls, and echo calls
   Across the haunted atmosphere,
With low, sweet laughs at intervals,—
   So reigns the rapture of the year.

Then ho! and hey! and whoop-hooray!
   Though winter clouds be looming,
Remember a November day
Is merrier than mildest May
   With all her blossoms blooming.

HONEY DRIPPING FROM THE COMB

How slight a thing may set one's fancy drifting
   Upon the dead sea of the Past!—A view—
Sometimes an odor—or a rooster lifting
      A far-off *"Ooh! ooh-ooh!"*

And suddenly we find ourselves astray
   In some wood's-pasture of the Long Ago—
Or idly dream again upon a day
      Of rest we used to know.

I bit an apple but a moment since—
   A wilted apple that the worm had spurned,—
Yet hidden in the taste were happy hints
      Of good old days returned.—

And so my heart, like some enraptured lute,
   Tinkles a tune so tender and complete,
God's blessing must be resting on the fruit—
      So bitter, yet so sweet!

BILLY COULD RIDE

I

BILLY was born for a horse's back!—
That's what Grandfather used to say:—
He'd seen him in dresses, a-many a day,
On a two-year-old, in the old barn-lot,
Prancing around, with the bridle slack,
And his two little sunburnt legs outshot
So straight from the saddle-seat you'd swear
A spirit-level had plumbed him there!
And all the neighbors that passed the place
Would just haul up in the road and stare
To see the little chap's father boost
The boy up there on his favorite roost,
To canter off, with a laughing face.—
Put him up there, he was satisfied—
And O the way that Billy could ride!

BILLY COULD RIDE

II

At celebration or barbecue—
And Billy, a boy of fifteen years—
Couldn't he cut his didoes there?—
What else would you expect him to,
On his little mettlesome chestnut mare,
With her slender neck, and her pointed ears,
And the four little devilish hooves of hers?
The "delegation" moved too slow
For the time that Billy wanted to go!
And to see him dashing out of the line
At the edge of the road and down the side
Of the long procession, all laws defied,
And the fife and drums, was a sight divine
To the girls, in their white-and-spangled pride
Wearily waving their scarfs about
In the great "Big Wagon," all gilt without
And jolt within, as they lumbered on
Into the town where Billy had gone
An hour ahead, like a knightly guide—
O but the way that Billy could ride!

BILLY COULD RIDE

III

"Billy can ride! Oh, Billy can ride!
But what on earth can he do beside?"
That's what the farmers used to say,
As time went by a year at a stride,
And Billy was twenty if he was a day!
And many a wise old father's foot
Was put right down where it should be put
While many a dutiful daughter sighed
In vain for one more glorious ride
With the gallant Billy, who none the less
Smiled at the old man's selfishness
And kissed his daughter, and rode away,—
Touched his horse in the flank—and *zipp!*-
Talk about horses and horsemanship!—
Folks stared after him just wild-eyed. . . .
Oomh! the way that Billy could ride!

SHE "DISPLAINS" IT

"Had, too!"
　"*Hadn't, neither!*"
So contended Bess and May—
　Neighbor children, who were boasting
Of their grandmammas, one day.

"Had, too!"
　"Hadn't, neither!"
All the difference begun
　By May's saying she'd *two* grandmas—
While poor Bess had only one.

"Had, too!"
　"Hadn't, neither!"
Tossing curls, and kinks of friz!—
　"How could you have *two* gran'muvvers
When ist *one* is all they is?"

"Had, too!"
　"Hadn't, neither!—
'Cause ef you had *two*," said Bess,
　"You'd *displain* it!" Then May answered
"*My* gran'mas wuz *twins*, I guess!"

THE WAY THE BABY SLEPT

This is the way the baby slept:
   A mist of tresses backward thrown
By quavering sighs where kisses crept
   With yearnings she had never known:
The little hands were closely kept
   About a lily newly blown—
And God was with her. And we wept.—
And this is the way the baby slept.

THE JOLLY MILLER

[Restored Romaunt]

It was a Jolly Miller lived on the River Dee;
He looked upon his piller, and there he found a flea;
"O Mr. Flea! you have bit me,
    And you shall shorely die!"
So he scrunched his bones ag'inst the stones—
    And there he let him lie!

'Twas then the Jolly Miller he laughed and told his wife,
And *she* laughed fit to kill her, and dropped her carving-knife!—
"O Mr. Flea!" "Ho-ho!" "Tee-hee!"
    They *both* laughed fit to kill,
Until the sound did almost drownd
    The rumble of the mill!

THE JOLLY MILLER

"Laugh on, my Jolly Miller! and Missus Miller,
    too!—
But there's a weeping-willer will soon wave over
    you!"
The voice was all so awful small—
    So very small and slim!—
He durst' infer that it was her,
    Ner her infer 'twas him!

That night the Jolly Miller, says he, "It's, Wifey
    dear,
That cat o' yourn, I'd kill her!—her actions is so
    queer,—
She's rubbin' 'g'inst the grindstone-legs,
    And yowlin' at the sky—
And I 'low the moon hain't greener
    Than the yaller of her eye!"

And as the Jolly Miller went chuckle-un to bed,
Was *Somepin'* jerked his piller from underneath
    his head!
"O Wife," says he, on-easi-lee,
    "Fetch here that lantern there!"
But *Somepin'* moans in thunder-tones,
    "*You tetch it ef you dare!*"

THE JOLLY MILLER

'Twas then the Jolly Miller he trimbled and he
  quailed—
And his wife choked until her breath come back,
  'n' she *wailed!*
And " *O!* " cried she, "it is *the Flea*,
  All white and pale and wann—
He's got you in his clutches, and
  He's bigger than a man!"

"*Ho! ho! my Jolly Miller*" (*fer 'twas the Flea,
  fer shore!*),
"*I reckon you'll not rack my bones ner scrunch
  'em any more!*"
Then *the Flea-Ghost* he grabbed him clos't,
  With many a ghastly smile,
And from the door-step stooped and hopped
  About four hundred mile!

WITH THE CURRENT

RAREST mood of all the year!
  Aimless, idle, and content—
Sky and wave and atmosphere
    Wholly indolent.

Little daughter, loose the band
  From your tresses—let them pour
Shadow-like o'er arm and hand
    Idling at the oar.

Low and clear, and pure and deep,
  Ripples of the river sing—
Water-lilies, half asleep,
    Drowsed with listening:

Tremulous reflex of skies—
  Skies above and skies below,—
Paradise and Paradise
    Blending even so!

WITH THE CURRENT

Blossoms with their leaves unrolled
    Laughingly, as they were lips
Cleft with ruddy beaten gold
        Tongues of pollen-tips.

Rush and reed, and thorn and vine,
    Clumped with grasses lithe and tall—
With a web of summer-shine
        Woven round it all.

Back and forth, and to and fro—
    Flashing scale and wing as one,—
Dragon-flies that come and go,
        Shuttled by the sun.

Fairy lilts and lullabies,
    Fine as fantasy conceives,—
Echoes wrought of cricket-cries
        Sifted through the leaves.

O'er the rose, with drowsy buzz,
    Hangs the bee, and stays his kiss,
Even as my fancy does,
        Gypsy, over this.

WITH THE CURRENT

Let us both be children—share
   Youth's glad voyage night and day
Drift adown it, half aware,
      Anywhere we may.—

Drift and curve and deviate,
   Veer and eddy, float and flow,
Waver, swerve and undulate,
      As the bubbles go.

A SLEEPING BEAUTY

I

An alien wind that blew and blew
Over the fields where the ripe grain grew,

Sending ripples of shine and shade
That crept and crouched at her feet and played

The sea-like summer washed the moss
Till the sun-drenched lilies hung like floss,

Draping the throne of green and gold
That lulled her there like a queen of old.

II

Was it the hum of a bumblebee,
Or the long-hushed bugle eerily

Winding a call to the daring Prince
Lost in the wood long ages since?—

A SLEEPING BEAUTY

A dim old wood, with a palace rare
Hidden away in its depths somewhere!

Was it the Princess, tranced in sleep,
Awaiting her lover's touch to leap

Into the arms that bent above?—
To thaw his heart with the breath of love—

And cloy his lips, through her waking tears
With the dead-ripe kiss of a hundred years!

III

An alien wind that blew and blew.—
I had blurred my eyes as the artists do,

Coaxing life to a half-sketched face,
Or dreaming bloom for a grassy place.

The bee droned on in an undertone;
And a shadow-bird trailed all alone

Across the wheat, while a liquid cry
Dripped from above, as it went by.

A SLEEPING BEAUTY

What to her was the far-off whir
Of the quail's quick wing or the chipmunk's chirr?—

What to her was the shade that slid
Over the hill where the reapers hid?—

Or what the hunter, with one foot raised,
As he turned to go—yet, pausing, gazed?

AT AUNTY'S HOUSE

One time, when we'z at Aunty's house—
   'Way in the country!—where
They's ist but woods—an' pigs, an' cows-
   An' all's outdoors an' air!—
An' orchurd-swing; an' churry-trees—
An' *churries* in 'em!—Yes, an' these-
Here redhead birds steals all they please,
   An' tetch 'em ef you dare!—
W'y, wunst, one time, when we wuz there
     We et out on the porch!

Wite where the cellar door wuz shut
   The table wuz; an' I
Let Aunty set by me an' cut
   My vittuls up—an' pie.
'Tuz awful funny!—I could see
The redheads in the churry-tree;
An' beehives, where you got to be
   So keerful, goin' by;—
An' "Comp'ny" there an' all!—an' we—
     We et out on the porch!

AT AUNTY'S HOUSE

An' I ist et *p'surves* an' things
   'At Ma don't 'low me to—
An' *chickun-gizzurds*—(don't like *wings*
   Like *Parunts* does! do *you?*)
An' all the time the wind blowed there,
An' I could feel it in my hair,
An' ist smell clover *ever*'where!—
   An' a' old redhead flew
Purt' nigh wite over my high-chair,
   When we et on the porch!

THE WHITHERAWAYS

[*Set Sail, October* 15, 1890]

THE Whitheraways!—That's what I'll have to call
You—sailing off, with never a word at all
Of parting!—sailing 'way across the sea,
With never one good-bye to *me*—to ME!

Sailing away from me, with no farewell!—
Ah, Parker Hitt and sister Muriel—
And Rodney, too, and little Laurance—all
Sailing away—just as the leaves, this Fall!

Well, then, *I* too shall sail on cheerily
As now you all go sailing o'er the sea:
I've *other* little friends with me on shore—
Though they but make me yearn for *you* the more!

And so, sometime, dear little friends afar,
When this faint voice shall reach you, and you are
All just a little homesick, you must be
As brave as I am now, and think of me!

THE WHITHERAWAYS

Or, haply, if your eyes, as mine, droop low,
And would be humored with a tear or so,—
Go to your *Parents*, Children!—let *them* do
The *crying*—'twill be easier for them to!

THE RAGGEDY MAN

O THE Raggedy Man! He works fer Pa;
An' he's the goodest man ever you saw!
He comes to our house every day,
An' waters the horses, an' feeds 'em hay;
An' he opens the shed—an' we all ist laugh
When he drives out our little old wobble-ly calf
An' nen—ef our hired girl says he can—
He milks the cow fer 'Lizabuth Ann.—
　Aint he a' awful good Raggedy Man?
　　Raggedy! Raggedy! Raggedy Man!

W'y, The Raggedy Man—he's ist so good
He splits the kindlin' an' chops the wood;
An' nen he spades in our garden, too,
An' does most things 'at boys can't do.—
He clumbed clean up in our big tree
An' shooked a' apple down fer me—
An' nother'n, too, fer 'Lizabuth Ann—
An' nother'n', too, fer The Raggedy Man.—
　Aint he a' awful kind Raggedy Man?
　　Raggedy! Raggedy! Raggedy Man!

THE RAGGEDY MAN

An' The Raggedy Man, he knows most rhymes
An' tells 'em, ef I be good, sometimes:
Knows 'bout Giunts, an' Griffuns, an' Elves,
An' the Squidgicum-Squees 'at swallers ther-
    selves!
An', wite by the pump in our pasture-lot,
He showed me the hole 'at the Wunks is got,
'At lives 'way deep in the ground, an' can
Turn into me, er' Lizabuth Ann!
  Aint he a funny old Raggedy Man?
    Raggedy! Raggedy! Raggedy Man!

The Raggedy Man—one time when he
Was makin' a little bow-'n'-orry fer me,
Says "When *you're* big like your Pa is,
Air you go' to keep a fine store like his—
An' be a rich merchunt—an' wear fine clothes?—
Er what *air* you go' to be, goodness knows!"
An' nen he laughed at 'Lizabuth Ann,
An' I says "'M go' to be a Raggedy Man!—
  I'm ist go' to be a nice Raggedy Man!"
    Raggedy! Raggedy! Raggedy Man!

A BOY'S MOTHER

My Mother she's so good to me,
Ef I was good as I could be,
I couldn't be as good—no, sir!—
Can't any boy be good as her!

She loves me when I'm glad er sad;
She loves me when I'm good er bad;
An', what's a funniest thing, she says
She loves me when she punishes.

I don't like her to punish me.—
That don't hurt,—but it hurts to see
Her cryin'.—Nen *I* cry; an' nen
We both cry an' be good again.

She loves me when she cuts an' sews
My little cloak an' Sund'y clothes;
An' when my Pa comes home to tea,
She loves him most as much as me.

She laughs an' tells him all I said,
An' grabs me up an' pats my head;
An' I hug *her*, an' hug my Pa
An' love him purt' nigh as much as Ma

IN SWIMMING-TIME

Clouds above, as white as wool,
    Drifting over skies as blue
As the eyes of beautiful
    Children when they smile at you:
Groves of maple, elm, and beech,
    With the sunshine sifted through
Branches, mingling each with each,
    Dim with shade and bright with dew

Stripling trees, and poplars hoar,
Hickory and sycamore,
And the drowsy dogwood, bowed
Where the ripples laugh aloud,
And the crooning creek is stirred
    To a gaiety that now
Mates the warble of the bird.
    Teetering on the hazel-bough.

IN SWIMMING-TIME

Grasses long and fine and fair
As your schoolboy-sweetheart's hair
Backward stroked and twirled and twined
By the fingers of the wind:
Vines and mosses interlinked
    Down dark aisles and deep ravines,
Where the stream runs, willow-brinked,
    Round a bend where some one leans,
Faint, and vague, and indistinct
    As the like-reflected thing
    In the current shimmering.

Childish voices, further on,
Where the truant stream has gone,
Vex the echoes of the wood
Till no word is understood—
Save that we are well aware
Happiness is hiding there:—
There, in leafy coverts, nude
    Little bodies poise and leap,
Spattering the solitude
And the silence, everywhere—
    Mimic monsters of the deep!—

IN SWIMMING-TIME

Wallowing in sandy shoals—
    Plunging headlong out of sight,
    And, with spurtings of delight,
Clutching hands, and slippery soles,
    Climbing up the treacherous steep,
Over which the spring-board spurns
Each again as he returns!
Ah! the glorious carnival!
    Purple lips—and chattering teeth—
    Eyes that burn—But, in beneath,
Every care beyond recall—
    Every task forgotten quite—
    And again in dreams at night,
Dropping, drifting through it all!

THE FISHING PARTY

Wunst we went a-fishin'—Me
An' my Pa an' Ma all three,
When they was a pic-nic, 'way
Out to Hanch's Woods, one day

An' they was a crick out there,
Where the fishes is, an' where
Little boys 'taint big an' strong,
Better have their folks along!

My Pa he ist fished an' fished!
An' my Ma she said she wished
Me an' her was home; an' Pa
Said he wished so worse'n Ma.

Pa said ef you talk, er say
Anything, er sneeze, er play,
Hain't no fish, alive er dead,
Ever go' to bite! he said.

THE FISHING PARTY

Purt' nigh dark in town when we
Got back home; an' Ma says she,
Now she'll have a fish fer shore!
An' she buyed one at the store.

Nen at supper, Pa he won't
Eat no fish, an' says he don't
Like 'em.—An' he pounded me
When I choked! . . . Ma, didn't he?

THE BOY LIVES ON OUR FARM

The Boy lives on our Farm, he's not
    Afeard o' horses none!
An' he can make 'em lope, er trot,
    Er rack, er pace, er run.
Sometimes he drives two horses, when
    He comes to town an' brings
A wagon-full o' 'taters nen,
    An' roastin'-ears an' things.

Two horses is "a team," he says,—
    An' when you drive er hitch,
The right-un's a "near-horse," I guess
    Er "off"—I don't know which.—
The Boy lives on our Farm, he told
    Me, too, 'at he can see,
By lookin' at their teeth, how old
    A horse is, to a T!

THE BOY LIVES ON OUR FARM

I'd be the gladdest boy alive
    Ef I knowed much as that,
An' could stand up like him an' drive
    An' ist push back my hat,
Like he comes skallyhootin' through
    Our alley, with one arm
A-wavin' Fare-ye-well! to you—
    The Boy lives on our Farm!

THE RUNAWAY BOY

Wunst I sassed my Pa, an' he
Won't stand that, an' punished me,—
Nen when he was gone that day,
I slipped out an' runned away.

I tooked all my copper-cents,
An' clumbed over our back fence
In the jimpson-weeds 'at growed
Ever'where all down the road.

Nen I got out there, an' nen
I runned some—an' runned again
When I met a man 'at led
A big cow 'at shooked her head.

I went down a long, long lane
Where was little pigs a-play'n';
An' a grea'-big pig went "Booh!"
An' jumped up, an' skeered me too.

Nen I scampered past, an' they
Was somebody hollered "Hey!"
An' I ist looked ever'where,
An' they was nobody there.

THE RUNAWAY BOY

I *want* to, but I'm 'fraid to try
To go back. . . . An' by-an'-by,
Somepin' hurts my throat inside—
An' I want my Ma—an' cried.

Nen' a grea'-big girl come through
Where's a gate, an' telled me who
Am I? an' ef I tell where
My home's at she'll show me there.

But I couldn't ist but tell
What's my *name;* an' she says well
An' she tooked me up an' says
She know where I live, she guess.

Nen she telled me hug wite close
Round her neck!—an' off she goes
Skippin' up the street! An' nen
Purty soon I'm home again.

An' my Ma, when she kissed me,
Kissed the *big girl* too, an' *she*
Kissed me—ef I p'omise *shore*
I won't run away no more!

OUR HIRED GIRL

Our hired girl, she's 'Lizabuth Ann;
   An' she can cook best things to eat!
She ist puts dough in our pie-pan,
   An' pours in somepin' 'at's good and sweet,
An' nen she salts it all on top
With cinnamon; an' nen she'll stop
   An' stoop an' slide it, ist as slow,
In th' old cook-stove, so's 'twont slop
   An' git all spilled; nen bakes it, so
   It's custard pie, first thing you know!
      An' nen she'll say:
   "Clear out o' my way!
   They's time fer work, an' time fer play!—
      Take yer dough, an' run, Child; run!
      Er I cain't git no cookin' done!"

When our hired girl 'tends like she's mad,
   An' says folks got to walk the chalk
When *she's* around, er wisht they had,
   I play out on our porch an' talk

OUR HIRED GIRL

To th' Raggedy Man 'at mows our lawn;
An' he says "*Whew!*" an' nen leans on
   His old crook-scythe, and blinks his eyes
An' sniffs all round an' says,—"I swawn!
   Ef my old nose don't tell me lies,
   It 'pears like I smell custard-pies!"
      An' nen *he'll* say,—
" 'Clear out o' my way!
They's time fer work an' time fer play!
     Take yer dough, an' run, Child; run!
     Er *she* cain't git no cookin' done!' "

Wunst our hired girl, when she
   Got the supper, an' we all et,
An' it was night, an' Ma an' me
   An' Pa went wher' the "Social" met,—
An' nen when we come home, an' see
A light in the kitchen-door, an' we
   Heerd a maccordeun, Pa says "Lan'-
O'-Gracious! who can *her* beau be?"
An' I marched in, an' 'Lizabuth Ann
   Wuz parchin' corn fer the Raggedy Man!
     Better say
"Clear out o' the way!

OUR HIRED GIRL

They's time fer work, an' time fer play!
    Take the hint, an' run, Child; run!
    Er we cain't git no *courtin'* done!"

ENVOY

Many pleasures of Youth have been buoyantly sung—
   And, borne on the winds of delight, may they beat
With their palpitant wings at the hearts of the Young,
   And in bosoms of Age find as warm a retreat!—
Yet sweetest of all of the musical throng,
   Though least of the numbers that upward aspire,
Is the one rising now into wavering song,
   As I sit in the silence and gaze in the fire.

'Tis a Winter long dead that beleaguers my door
   And muffles his steps in the snows of the past:
And I see, in the embers I'm dreaming before,
   Lost faces of love as they looked on me last:—
The round, laughing eyes of the desk-mate of old
   Gleam out for a moment with truant desire—
Then fade and are lost in a City of Gold,
   As I sit in the silence and gaze in the fire.

ENVOY

And then comes the face, peering back in my own,
   Of a shy little girl, with her lids drooping low,
As she faltering tells, in a far-away tone,
   The ghost of a story of long, long ago.—
Then her dewy blue eyes they are lifted again;
   But I see their glad light slowly fail and expire,
As I reach and cry to her in vain, all in vain!—
   As I sit in the silence and gaze in the fire.

Then the face of a Mother looks back, through the mist
   Of the tears that are welling; and, lucent with light,
I see the dear smile of the lips I have kissed
   As she knelt by my cradle at morning and night;
And my arms are outheld, with a yearning too wild
   For any but God in His love to inspire,
As she pleads at the foot of His throne for her child,—
   As I sit in the silence and gaze in the fire.

O pathos of rapture! O glorious pain!
   My heart is a blossom of joy overrun

ENVOY

With a shower of tears, as a lily with rain
    That weeps in the shadow and laughs in the sun.
The blight of the frost may descend on the tree,
    And the leaf and the flower may fall and expire,
But ever and ever love blossoms for me,
    As I sit in the silence and gaze in the fire.